When Love Goes South

EMMA POWER

When
Love
Goes
South

A Guide
To Help You
Turn Conflict
Around

Hardie Grant

BOOKS

Beneath this hard shell of protection is your authentic self. This is who you truly are in your innermost being. The ego, however, builds itself so strongly, working so hard to preserve itself over the years, that most of us think that the ego *is* who we are. And it can be very hard to see beyond that layer.

In his book *A New Earth*, spiritual teacher and author Eckhart Tolle teaches us that nothing strengthens the ego more than feeling separate to others: 'Every ego is continuously struggling for survival, trying to protect and enlarge itself. To uphold the I-thought, it needs the opposite thought of "the other". The conceptual "I" cannot survive without the conceptual "other". The others are most others when I see them as my enemies.'

He also tells us that nothing feels better than making someone else wrong.

'There is nothing that strengthens the ego more than being right. Being right is identification with a mental position – a perspective, an opinion, a judgement, a story. For you to be right, of course, you need someone else to be wrong, and so the ego loves to make wrong in order to be right. In other words: you need to make others wrong in order to get a stronger sense of who you are ... Being right places you in a position of imagined moral superiority in relation to the person or situation that is being judged and found wanting. It is that sense of superiority the ego craves and through which it enhances itself.'

This is why it's essential to address the ego: how can we understand and better deal with conflict and challenges without an awareness of the huge part our ego plays?

Not only will the ego feel the need to point the finger, it will defend itself to the death. It is the part of us that is highly defensive, which is often the cause of arguments. It will flare at the first sign of anyone questioning our ideas, values or behaviours, and will reject those that don't align with our current worldview.

Once we begin to recognise the ego in ourselves, we'll also start to see how it operates in others. This can help us take their stuff less personally. We can notice when their ego feels under threat, which, of course, will cause them to have strong reactions – though I would avoid pointing this out in the moment. Nothing flares an ego more than being called out. If you feel you have to tell someone they're in their ego, it's most likely *your* ego needing to feel superior.

Awareness of ego brings more understanding as to why and how we are fighting.

The ego and how it gets involved

Each of us has an image of who we think we are. Our sense of self is made up of a collection of identifications we've gathered that feel like 'me'. This conditioned self, called the ego, starts to form in childhood. It begins with the reflection we receive from the people around us. As we grow, we continue to collect and learn patterns, beliefs, definitions, behaviours, constructs and judgements. We are told who we are, what we should feel and how we should think, by our families, the culture and the systems around us. We identify with how we look, what we own, our titles, and our perception of success or failure.

Essentially, our identity is based on this image of ourselves that we have absorbed and then built. The ego is what we perceive as 'I'. It's the voice in our head. Many people have very little or no awareness of the ego.

Think of the ego as a shield. Its purpose is to protect us from the outer world. It helps us to survive and, in order to do this, it needs to view everything outside of itself as separate to it. The sense of 'I' is what propels us to protect our body. It motivates us and gives us something to fight for.

'A lack of self-awareness is one of the greatest causes of conflict in relationships.'

Human nature isn't something we're really taught about, but it greatly influences our experience on this planet. Knowing how and why we operate in the way we do can make all the difference to our life journey. In this chapter, we'll begin to understand our nature and those of our loved ones. These aspects of who we are and how we behave constantly affect the quality of our connections. A lack of self-awareness is one of the greatest causes of conflict in relationships. So let's open up and delve deep as we get to know ourselves and our loved ones on a whole new level.

Understanding *Humans*

1

Why we do what we do

Becoming conscious during conflict requires us to change. It calls on us to be courageous and curious enough to question our history, patterns, communication style and personal reality. This process is going to be deep and demanding, but that's where you'll discover your relationship diamonds.

This guide is less self-help and more self-love. You're giving yourself the gift of rewarding relationships, whether they're with your partner, loved ones, colleagues or community. As you tuck these tools into your belt and take them into your interactions, you'll feel the exhilarating highs of transforming a challenging situation, conversation or troubled relationship waters. And you'll likely shock the people in your life with your new ability to handle the relational storms that come your way.

So, are you ready to rediscover connection through conflict, and bask in the beauty of your repaired relationships? Let's grow.

Introduction

A harmonious relationship can fight the good fight.

From frustrating arguments about emptying the dishwasher, through to intense disputes about money or sex, relationships inevitably hit bumps in the road. As you're about to discover, conflict can be one of the greatest opportunities for personal growth and relational depth.

It's how we choose to deal with these breakdowns that either sustains or starves our connections. We can push through, avoid the problem or make it worse. Or we can make peace with conflict and learn how to use it to strengthen and secure our relationships. By having each other's backs in the hard times, you'll get yourselves on track for more good times together.

Think of this guidebook as a map for your journey, carefully curated to give you the skills to go from breakdown to breakthrough. It's your recipe for ease, love and joy. Sure, you'll still have hard days and tricky phases, but you'll have the tools to guide you through.

You're about to discover the path from conflict to connection. Together, we'll look at simple hacks for preventing conflict, unpack the psychology and physiology of conflict, discover what to do in the heat of an argument – and how to find the gold afterwards.

Practice

Think of someone in your life who you have
a tendency to label or call names. Bastard,
bitch, selfish, arsehole ... you get the idea.

1. Notice how you want to hold onto that.
   Don't try and stop the feeling, just observe.
2. Turn the label into an 'I feel' statement. For
   example, instead of 'Susan is a controlling
   bitch', turn it into, 'When Susan tells me
   how to parent my children, I feel frustrated
   and belittled'. Don't judge your feelings.
   Simply acknowledge how the situation
   makes *you* feel. You're taking a moment
   here to look inwards instead of outwards.
3. Take the label you have given the person
   and simply add the question, 'Is this true?'
       'Susan is a controlling bitch.' ...
   'Is this true?'
       Susan may have controlling tendencies,
   but is her whole being that of a controlling
   bitch? When we are hurt or angry, we
   tend to make global accusations about
   the person's entire personality, instead
   of staying focused on the specific offence
   at hand.

will not feel good. And that's exactly how you know it's an ego squeeze. You will feel the bejesus being squeezed out of you as your ego throws a hissy fit at the very suggestion of making amends. It's an intense emotional and mental contraction. This can feel like you're facing a type of death, which is a very unnatural space to lean into. But if, in that moment, you step out of your comfort zone and attempt to make amends, not only are you more likely to reconcile with your loved one, but your ego will take a hit. (And remember, that is a good thing!)

If you manage to reach out to your loved one, regardless of that feeling of contraction, well done! Give yourself a massive pat on the back. (Just not too massive, or you'll blow your ego up all over again!)

The tendencies of the ego are interesting to observe. They take some vigilance to spot, as the ego can tell convincing stories. See this as an interesting or amusing exercise. Don't get disheartened when you spot your ego. It's not 'bad'; it's an essential aspect of the human experience. It has played an important role in your life and has been a necessary part of your evolution. Trying to be rid of it will only grow it further. Instead, simply play the game of watching it, and view your conflicts as an opportunity to give it a little squeeze.

EGO SQUEEZE

Battling against our own ego is a fruitless act. If we actively try to ignore it or stop it, it will likely weasel its way into another aspect of our identity and assert itself once more. However, there are certain choices we can make that will help lessen its grip over us. Conflict offers us a great opportunity for this. There are moments where we can choose to act in a way that deals a blow to our ego. Each time we do this, it loses power over us.

Enter the ego squeeze.

You know those moments where you're knee-deep in conflict? Or perhaps you're reliving a grievance from long ago. Every part of you is screaming, 'shut down, run, fight, throw your toys, hold onto your story'. You're pointing the finger and firing up. Or you're hurting and in pain. You're feeling about as separate from the other person as you can get. This is a crossroads, and it's an opportunity.

What if in that moment you go against all your conditioning and reach out to make amends? To make a move from separation to unity? To look at the situation from the other person's perspective, apologise for how you have contributed, vulnerably share the real hurt behind the fight or reach out with loving touch?

Reaching out for union when the ego thrives on separation isn't going to feel easy. The squeeze

REAL CHALLENGES VS. PERCEIVED CHALLENGES

Not every difference of opinion, difficult situation or conflict is your ego talking. Sometimes when someone is behaving in a problematic way or a troubling situation has arisen, things truly need
to be addressed. There's nothing heroic or spiritual about putting up with bad behaviour. And there's nothing wrong with addressing a mistake or fault with the intention to create change.

However, when we are faced with a challenge, it's important to ask ourselves: which part of this is the situation itself and which part is the voice of my ego?

We know when the ego is involved because it goes beyond the facts. Are you addressing the situation in the name of change, or are you there to make someone wrong? Are you enjoying the feeling of being right? Are you feeling defensive? Are you taking it personally? Are you identifying with your mental position? If you are name-calling, being self-righteous, bitching and complaining, you've tipped into ego. The situation may be real, but the ego is being opportunistic.

Your job here is to see if you can catch the moment of temptation. Even catching a small glimpse of your ego loosens its grip. Awareness of the ego is the conscious self-observing a pattern or tendency of the mind.

By simply investigating your statements, you might discover that there is more to the story. Nothing is black and white, and it's important to allow for the grey areas and multiple realities to co-exist. In simply questioning your own thoughts, a more creative answer may arise. This simple exercise can widen your lens.

'Susan isn't a controlling bitch, but her comments make me feel like she is trying to control me. When I zoom out, I can see that her behaviour comes from her own insecurities.'

Widening the lens doesn't make Susan's behaviour right, but it takes some of the charge out of the situation. It lets the ego step aside and allows the conscious self to acknowledge what's happening from a more neutral standpoint, and come up with a clearer solution. This might mean you simply don't take Susan's comments to heart. Or perhaps you might have a discussion with her from a non-charged position.

Try this

Notice the next time you label someone in the heat of the moment. Zoom out for a moment and apply the process described above. Rather than making a global criticism of their entire character, identify what it is that specifically bothers you.

WITNESS AWARENESS

Witness awareness is the part of us that is witness to the voice in our own head. While the ego identifies with our thoughts, emotions, inner monologue and opinions, the witness can think about what we are thinking about. The ego is automatic, while the witness is a level of consciousness that enables us to stand back and observe what is happening within us. It's a damn fine friend to have and to hone. Experiencing and developing our witness awareness is one of the most powerful ways we can deepen our connection with ourselves and our loved ones.

This is a major game-changer because the witness is *who we truly are*. It is our authentic self! Learning to have and use this awareness can bring a profound turning point in our lives, enabling us to have a truer and more honest relationship with ourselves. When we can separate the voice in our head from actual reality, we become conscious. And as we become *more* conscious, we become more free.

We still experience our thoughts and emotions. We still have opinions, beliefs and an internal monologue. But when we disengage from being so closely identified with these things, when we realise these things aren't *us*, we weaken their control over us. We step back and observe from a broader point of view, and with this new sense of the bigger picture, we take on an expanded perspective.

Imagine you are swimming in a turbulent ocean, getting thrown around by the waves, currents and swell. You then make your way to the beach. The wild activity in the ocean is still happening, but you can now watch it from the sand. That swirling ocean is your ego chatting away in your mind. And that person on the beach, observing at a distance, is your witness. When you manage to separate the two, you become less controlled by the contents of your mind, and you can also more easily question it. You begin to see where your thinking is dysfunctional, poisonous, irrelevant, distracting or unnecessary. You recognise where you are creating stories, making judgements and projecting onto others. You start to see how you have been conditioned by your culture and upbringing, and that you may have internalised beliefs that were never yours to begin with.

Now, you can not only question these things, but you can also start making choices that go beyond your conditioned thoughts and behaviour. This will enable you to witness your mind creating false assumptions or accusations, or taking things too personally. You'll have less need to defend yourself or jump to rash conclusions. You will be able to reflect on your own behaviour and allow new opinions to enter your awareness.

If these ideas are new to you, you may be feeling a little confronted right now. The ego is terrified of being exposed. Suggesting that you question your thoughts, emotions and beliefs may feel like an attack because, remember, the ego has us thinking that *we are* those things.

1: UNDERSTANDING HUMANS

But breathe deep, and remind yourself: 'I am safe to witness my feelings. I am safe to question my beliefs. I am safe to investigate my thoughts.'

For most people, awakening is a long-term process, a gradual unfolding. There will be moments of clarity and expansion, then you'll lose yourself again. You'll have experiences of consciousness, and then unconsciousness. But gradually, as you increase your awareness, certain traits, triggers, thought patterns and stories will start to fall away. Think of your psyche as a pond. Sometimes it's clear, and sometimes it gets stirred up and becomes murky. Our witness awareness is like a sieve, lifting sediment from the pond, leaving the water that much clearer.

Your job is to practice cultivating awareness. You don't need to change what you observe, just witness it with presence. As you do so, your ego will relax. Let's look at some practices that can help this process.

Emotions

One simple way to develop your witness awareness is through the observation of your emotions. Let's begin with the least confronting observation process – observing neutral or even pleasant feelings.

Practice

Take a minute, and ask yourself:

'What am I feeling right now?'
Describe it honestly and without judgement.
    'I am feeling _____ .'
    As you move through your day, take moments to regularly observe how you feel, and describe the feeling without attaching a story or judgement to it. As you're walking somewhere, sitting in a meeting, texting a friend, washing the dishes, think: 'I am feeling _____ .' Use the first words that come to mind.
    Next, try this in a situation where the feelings you experience are less than pleasant, or when you've been triggered.

'What am I really feeling right now?'
(Example: 'I am feeling anxious.')

How does your body feel?
(Example: 'My heart is beating fast and I'm finding it hard to breathe.')
    Witness how you are feeling emotionally without trying to change it. Observe how you are physically feeling, and allow it to be fully

there. Refrain from labelling your experience as 'bad', or suppressing it. Sit with the feelings that come up, without the interference of the mind, and simply be present.

Tip

Try to stay in the space of the observer for at least 90 seconds. This is how long emotions express themselves on a physiological level. Eventually, by staying with the feeling and simply witnessing it without judgement, you may find the clarity to guide yourself through the necessary steps to address the situation. MRI studies of the brain show that this process of observing calms the parts of our brain that regulate our heightened emotions, and therefore helps us re-centre. Remember, you are not trying to stop the emotion, but to let it naturally express and flow through your system.

Practice

Next time you see content that triggers you or riles you up, take a moment to witness how you are feeling, and observe, without judging or reacting, how it expresses itself in your physical body.

Advanced practice

Try the previous practice during a difficult conversation or fight. Although it is far more difficult to do this while with another person, if you've been doing this practice alone, you'll have flexed your witness muscles and it will come more naturally.

The people in our life aren't usually *intending* to emotionally trigger us. Think about a time when you said something that felt straightforward or innocent and the other person reacted strongly. You weren't deliberately trying to create a fight. You were just being you. It's important to recognise that being emotionally triggered in a relationship is inevitable. Our job is to observe our automatic and unconscious responses so we can dig a little deeper and discover the source.

Helpful questions to ask yourself in this moment include:

'Am I responding to the present or am I being triggered by my past?'

'How much of this is mine to own?'

PATTERNS

The way we relate in relationships and friendships is often cyclical. We repeat the same patterns, interactions and conflict scenarios. The context may look different, but the show plays out the same. Interestingly, we are often unaware of our repeated cycles. They are entrenched in history, a repetition of a model of behaviour we learned from a young age.

A client of mine, Cameron, came to see me because he was finding it hard to maintain friendships. He is a friendly, fun, outgoing person who finds it easy to meet new people. His connections were starting with a burst of good intent and the promise of many happy times to come. But not long after the initial excitement wore off, things would shift. He would automatically start to notice traits in his new friend that he found unfavourable. He had an uncanny knack for spotting their flaws, making him reluctant to engage in the relationship, and he would ultimately ghost or bail on them. Cameron's experience was due to a combination of an overactive negativity bias and a lack of grace. The irony was that Cameron did, in fact, yearn for deep friendships, and kept wondering why there wasn't anyone out there worth being friends with!

As we explored the pattern, Cameron revealed that he had never felt worthy in his father's eyes. It had felt impossible to gain his dad's approval, as it seemed like the bar was constantly being raised. As we discussed this pattern, a lightbulb went off for Cameron. He realised he'd been repeating this pattern in his friendships – raising his standards so high no-one could ever meet them.

Awareness and reflection bring consciousness to our patterns. This won't necessarily shift them immediately – patterns are often deeply entrenched, which means they don't die easily. But observation will give you the clarity to see where and how they're in operation. You can then call them out and take small steps towards a new way of doing things.

Cameron made a commitment to practice grace and gratitude in his connections, taking note of what he *did* like and what *was* working. He committed to giving his friendships more of a chance before he bailed on them. And it worked – he made and maintained connections that lasted.

'Awareness and reflection bring consciousness to our patterns.'

Practice

Take a moment to observe a pattern that repeats itself in your life. Perhaps it is in the types of relationships you have, or have had. Maybe it's in a conflict scenario that continues to show up in a close relationship. Describe it honestly, without judgement.

'The pattern I have observed is _____.'
Next, ask yourself why you think this is happening.
'I think this pattern repeats itself because _____.' (It's okay if you don't know the answer.)
Reflect on any ways you think you contribute to the cycle.
'My contribution to this pattern repeating itself is _____.'

(**NOTE:** sometimes your contribution isn't specific to the pattern, but staying in the scenario in which the pattern occurs is the thing you're doing to repeat it.)

And finally, what's one small step you can take to shift this pattern?
'I commit to _____.'

STORIES

The ego is a skilful storyteller. When it comes to conflict or disharmony in a relationship, our minds will often jump straight into a story – about ourselves, about the other person, about the relationship itself. These stories are usually about how a situation *should* be, and how someone *should* have behaved in it. This puts us at odds with life as it actually is.

It's important to recognise that our stories are simply that – stories. Ironically, if we believe them and keep telling them to ourselves and others, they are more likely to become our reality. Like a magnifying glass, we amplify the aspects we focus on. Our stories shape our life experience – if they take hold, our lives will often come to reflect the script we are writing.

As noted earlier, the physiological experience of emotions as sensation in the body lasts for approximately 90 seconds. What keeps emotions persisting beyond that are the stories we spin in our heads. It's in the mind that the pain continues to live, rather than in the situation. This can have our emotions running for days, months, or even years. We relive the experience in our body every time we revive the story from the past.

'What keeps emotions persisting are the stories we spin in our heads.'

Some examples of stories we might tell ourselves include:

- 'He's late because I'm not a priority to him.'
- 'She's not answering her phone because she's lying about where she is.'
- 'This relationship will end just like the last one did.'
- 'They never loved me anyway.'
- 'He hasn't texted me because he's upset with me.'

Sometimes these stories might be true, or they might possess a snippet of truth. But sometimes they're a total fairytale, existing only in our imagination.

NOTE: If you're having trouble deciphering the difference between your intuition and a story, it can be helpful to speak with a trusted friend, therapist or, if appropriate, the person your story is about. The idea here is not to go against your instincts, but to honestly determine where drama or the past is influencing your current reality.

Tip

Next time you're challenged, home in and observe the story you've attached to the situation.

'What story am I telling myself right now? Is this story true?'

Observe how, when and why you tell the story – to yourself and others – and whether you're doing this over and over.

SHADOW

The shadow is a psychological term for the parts of ourselves we have unconsciously disowned. Our shadow is filled with traits and tendencies we don't want to acknowledge or admit to – even to ourselves. This pool of 'stuff' we've collected follows us around, even if we don't know it's there. Yet.

We go to great lengths to protect our self-image from what we deem to be negative characteristics, building up our shadow in the process. However, in doing this, we are avidly protecting – and preventing – ourselves from fully knowing ourselves as whole, integrated beings.

We ignore or repress these parts because – usually from childhood onwards – we tend to perceive certain traits or emotions as unattractive, unlovable or 'bad'. When we first expressed these thoughts, ideas or traits – or when we first witnessed someone else expressing them – they were met with a negative reaction, or perhaps rejection. And so, we learn to suppress these parts of ourselves, out of a deep-seated fear of being rejected.

This repression can create problems in our relationships that may provoke the very rejection we're trying to avoid. These disowned, unexamined parts of ourselves don't just disappear, they become part of our unconscious, split off from our awareness. Without this awareness, they rear up and express themselves in destructive ways, often erupting seemingly from out of nowhere, or playing out in unhealthy choices and behaviours.

Rather than face our suppressed shadow tendencies, we often seek to ease our discomfort by projecting them onto others. We accuse others of having the very traits we are hiding deep within us. The negative characteristic we perceive in others may not be there at all. Or perhaps there's an element of it within them, but we amplify it. Often the reason we're so quick to notice it is because it already exists within us, and the reason it triggers us so strongly is because we haven't resolved it within ourselves.

We also have a tendency to project onto others if we are feeling unhappy or uncomfortable. Instead of observing and addressing these feelings in ourselves, we point the finger, blaming those around us for the pain we feel.

I witnessed this process firsthand when my clients Chiara and Tristan first came to see me. Chiara was at her wit's end. She felt like Tristan was constantly accusing her of things that he himself was actually doing, from small things like not cleaning up after herself to bigger things like not listening during their conversations. He also seemed intent on constantly pointing out what he perceived as her character flaws. Chiara felt like she was constantly on the defensive, trying to prove herself as a person and show that she wasn't doing the things he was accusing her of doing. Tristan was clearly unhappy, but refused to admit it and was instead blaming her. Chiara felt like she was walking on eggshells, that there was nothing she could do to make Tristan happy – and she was right. The couple kept moving from one fight to the next, until their relationship reached breaking point.

We tend to project in this way because we haven't properly learnt to sit with our pain. This starts when we're young. Quite often, when a child is upset, they get handed a screen or sweets to distract them from themselves. We're not used to handling our pain unaided, so we learn to project onto others or seek methods that help us numb out. When we do this, however, we're not healing the shadow or even exploring it; we're perpetuating its existence. It will lie dormant, ready to erupt at the next opportunity in a recurring pattern of emotional reactivity. Introducing witness awareness to our shadow gives us the opportunity to have an honest look at it. To do this, we need a solid dose of acceptance and non-judgement. We won't dare to take a proper look at ourselves if we're terrified of what the voice in our head will have to say about what we see. This is why, when it comes to exploring our shadow, self-compassion is just as essential as self-responsibility.

Let's go lovingly, like you would with a child who was dealing with a difficult emotion. Take yourself by the hand and gently lead yourself into that deep, dark cave that appears so scary. The cave of 'unacceptable' feelings, emotions, ideas and behaviours.

Witness your shadow. Be radically honest with yourself and admit to those hidden traits and thoughts. You may do this in the quiet of the night, while standing in the shower, during a meditation, or even in a moment of conflict. If the voice of judgement shows up, witness that too. By shining the light of awareness and acceptance into all the corners, you'll illuminate what was scary. It loses charge every time it's exposed.

Observing our shadow without judgement allows us to build a healthy relationship with every part of ourselves. This builds self-acceptance, which is a crucial element of self-love. To truly love someone else requires us to know them and radically accept them. The same goes for ourselves. When we own our shadow, we *really* get to know ourselves. And it's only when we fully know ourselves that we can experience true self-love. When we own all sides of ourselves, we become more integrated, and can express our shadow traits in a healthier way. We learn to meet them and integrate them and, quite often, the source of the emotions will reveal itself. Whether it's jealousy, anger, selfishness, desire, greed, deep sadness, fear, or any other perceived 'negative' trait. If each of us practiced deep ownership of our shadow selves, we would do far less damage to our connections.

This is what eventually happened for my client, Tristan. He was able to finally recognise he had been living with a deep unhappiness for years. To anyone on the outside, he had seemed like a happy guy, the life of the party. Although some activities, like playing sport, would create a temporary fix, nothing solved his problem in the long-term. Tristan couldn't bear to sit with his inner pain and unhappiness, and he also couldn't bear to examine its cause. So he believed that if he was unhappy, it must be someone else's fault. Chiara, being the closest person to him, was an easy target to blame.

As Tristan started to look at parts of his life, particularly his childhood, that weren't as happy as he had long convinced himself they were, he slowly became aware of the source of his pain. After uncovering and examining the feelings he had been repressing, he no longer needed to blame Chiara for his unhappiness. From this place of awareness, he was able to deeply apologise and begin a process of healing.

Tristan managed to do the work needed to save his marriage, but I've seen many other relationships break down over the projection of someone's shadow self. Being on the receiving end of someone's projection can feel extremely confusing, upsetting and overwhelming, because you're being accused of the very things that exist in the other person; the parts of themselves they refuse to own, or the pain they don't want to acknowledge.

It is better for all of us to have our shadow self on the table without judgement, otherwise the shadow will be expressed in more subtle, underhanded and, ultimately, unhealthy ways. Again, this comes down to the bravery to express them.

Practice

It's time to explore your shadow, without judgement.

- Take note the next time you feel tempted to point the finger when you don't feel very good within yourself. Ask yourself: 'What am I lacking right now that could be the real reason behind this feeling?' Perhaps you're feeling sleep-deprived, irritable or depressed. The easy way out is to blame someone else for your mood. When you step back and witness, you'll be able to get to the source of your discomfort and take action, rather than causing more tension. Perhaps the solution is getting help, or taking time for self-care.
- Tap into *how* you think. Is there a particular way that you think that you would never want anyone to know about?
- Think of someone who creates strong reactivity in you. Can you see any correlation between some of the things you don't like about them and the things you don't want anyone to know about you?
- Question your finger pointing. As we learned about the ego, sometimes there is an actual situation occurring, but sometimes it's simply our own issues getting in the way.

I had a client who experienced a painful childhood, particularly in his relationship with his mother. While growing up, he was exposed to intense manipulation, severe emotional reactivity and abandonment. As he grew in self-awareness, he recognised that he had a tendency to push partners to the point where they would behave in certain ways that confirmed his story about women. So when he started a new relationship, he was determined to change his pattern. He shared his background and resulting tendency with his new girlfriend. He then went on to offer her a game plan. 'I'm working on changing, and I encourage your feedback. If you ever notice me pushing your buttons or trying to get a reaction out of you, please help me become aware of what I'm doing.' They then came up with a code statement they could use when she felt this was happening.

Can you think of examples where you confirm your own stories by pushing someone into their shadow? Have you ever felt like you're on the receiving end of this dynamic?

The way we behave is our own responsibility. No-one *makes* us do anything. They merely expose a wound, story or belief we have yet to examine or question.

Our reactions are a helpful compass to guide us towards the areas we most need to observe within ourselves. Witness your own reactivity and regard it as a personal signpost. When you have a strong reaction see it as a sign to go inwards, before launching into battle.

When we react, we're in resistance to reality. We're refusing to accept what is happening in the present moment. Our ideals are being shaken and our ego is squeezing. We are fighting against life. When we do this, we expend all of our energy in the battle.

But if we pause and enter a state of awareness, we call our energy back to us. This newly available energy can then be used to respond from a deeper, inner source. True spiritual growth comes from the practice of creating space from our incessant mental and emotional activity. It is learning where we can let go.

This doesn't mean we become passive. Don't get me wrong – injustice does exist, and there is nothing wrong with challenging the thoughts, rules and beliefs of others. In fact, bringing consciousness to injustice is to be in integrity.

When we observe injustices from our witness viewpoint, we still take action, but it is action borne out of awareness. If we come from a place of reaction, our response is more likely to be toxic. If we come from a place of awareness, we are able to tap into the most truly conscious and appropriate response.

Ego Self vs Conscious Self

Let's take a look at some of the differences between our Ego Self and our Conscious Self.

Ego Self

- Feels under threat when it is questioned.
- Name-calls.
- Seeks opportunities for drama, pain, conflict.
- Complains.
- Takes the behaviour of others personally.
- Holds long-term resentments and grievances.
- Considers its thoughts to be itself.
- Unconsciously repeats patterns and behaviours.
- Creates stories of victimhood.
- Is highly defensive.
- Is highly reactive.
- Needs to prove itself.
- Blames others when feeling painful emotions.
- Denies another person's reality.
- Perceives different opinions as a threat.
- Is extremely rigid.
- Is in constant comparison to others.
- Is in constant judgement of others and itself.
- Will continue to look outwards so it can avoid looking inwards.

Tip

Be a safe person for your loved ones to reveal
their hidden traits or confronting feelings to.
When a loved one discloses an aspect of their
shadow self or shares a vulnerable truth, try to witness
and listen without judgement. In doing so, you show
them it's safe for them to reveal themselves to you,
which will encourage further revelations and an
authentic connection. This may mean you need to
breathe through your reactions, particularly if their
truths reveal something that triggers you or
is painful for you to receive. A client of mine, Chris,
was questioning his marriage to his wife Katie. When
he eventually shared his feelings to Katie, he fully
expected her to react strongly. Instead, she listened
to how he felt and stayed open to his perspective.
Although his revelation was incredibly painful to
receive, rather than shaming or blaming him, she
responded by saying that although this truth hurt her
to hear, she was grateful for his honesty. This gave
them an opportunity to problem-solve together from
a calm space. They then turned to relationship
coaching to work on rebuilding their connection.

BELIEFS

Each of us holds an image of how we think life *should* look. We have ideals about how things are meant to be, based on beliefs we may never have questioned.

We rarely interrogate our beliefs about the world or our ideas around relationships, because they are so deeply ingrained that we assume they must be right. We rarely even *think* to question what we believe.

Because of these unquestioned beliefs, we struggle. Our beliefs are an intrinsic aspect of the ego. We fight or reject the reality we experience when we compare it to the fantasy we hold in our head, or when we butt up against a different belief to our own.

When we take a step back from our beliefs and observe them from the perspective of the witness, this allows us to entertain the possibility of a different viewpoint. We question how we've been programmed, which then enables us to question our beliefs, update them if necessary, and ultimately live a life that is in keeping with beliefs that resonate with us; beliefs we want to call our own.

Our beliefs deeply affect our behaviour. I was brought up in a very religious household. I am grateful for the spiritual insight I received throughout my upbringing, but I can't say that the structured religion resonated strongly with me personally. For some years, I lived with a cognitive dissonance between the beliefs I'd been taught and the intuitive experience of my own relationship to spirituality. By asking myself the scary question – do I really think this is true? – I had to face my fears around everything I had been taught.

It felt scary because it was a type of death – my ego letting go of what it had identified with, and as, for so very long. I feared damage to my family relationships, and the loss of connection to some of my friends at the time. But rarely does anyone regret following their truest intuition.

This isn't something I have experienced in isolation. I have witnessed many of my clients improve their relationship with themselves and others by letting go of various learned beliefs and embracing their true beliefs.

'We fight or reject the reality we experience when we compare it to the fantasy we hold in our head.'

1: UNDERSTANDING HUMANS

Practice

What are some of the sayings or messages you were brought up with? For example:

'Women should behave like ...'
'Men should behave like ...'
'Relationships are hard work.'
'The man is the head of the household.'
'The people in our family are ...'

Do you still believe these sayings to be true?
What are some of the long-held beliefs that you were brought up with about relationships? Consider the influence that society, religion or the media has had on you. Do you still consider these beliefs to be true?
Are there beliefs you would like to let go of? If so, what is stopping you?

Tip

It's important to remember that multiple realities can exist at once. Just because a belief is no longer true for you doesn't mean it's not true for someone else.

Ego Self vs Conscious Self

Let's take a look at some of the differences between our Ego Self and our Conscious Self.

Ego Self

- Feels under threat when it is questioned.
- Name-calls.
- Seeks opportunities for drama, pain, conflict.
- Complains.
- Takes the behaviour of others personally.
- Holds long-term resentments and grievances.
- Considers its thoughts to be itself.
- Unconsciously repeats patterns and behaviours.
- Creates stories of victimhood.
- Is highly defensive.
- Is highly reactive.
- Needs to prove itself.
- Blames others when feeling painful emotions.
- Denies another person's reality.
- Perceives different opinions as a threat.
- Is extremely rigid.
- Is in constant comparison to others.
- Is in constant judgement of others and itself.
- Will continue to look outwards so it can avoid looking inwards.

The way we behave is our own responsibility. No-one *makes* us do anything. They merely expose a wound, story or belief we have yet to examine or question.

Our reactions are a helpful compass to guide us towards the areas we most need to observe within ourselves. Witness your own reactivity and regard it as a personal signpost. When you have a strong reaction see it as a sign to go inwards, before launching into battle.

When we react, we're in resistance to reality. We're refusing to accept what is happening in the present moment. Our ideals are being shaken and our ego is squeezing. We are fighting against life. When we do this, we expend all of our energy in the battle.

But if we pause and enter a state of awareness, we call our energy back to us. This newly available energy can then be used to respond from a deeper, inner source. True spiritual growth comes from the practice of creating space from our incessant mental and emotional activity. It is learning where we can let go.

This doesn't mean we become passive. Don't get me wrong – injustice does exist, and there is nothing wrong with challenging the thoughts, rules and beliefs of others. In fact, bringing consciousness to injustice is to be in integrity.

When we observe injustices from our witness viewpoint, we still take action, but it is action borne out of awareness. If we come from a place of reaction, our response is more likely to be toxic. If we come from a place of awareness, we are able to tap into the most truly conscious and appropriate response.

Conscious Self

- Doesn't take the behaviour of others personally.
- Seeks opportunities for union.
- Has awareness of personal patterns and behaviours.
- Communicates from a place of presence.
- Doesn't make assumptions.
- Listens to intuition to find creative solutions.
- Has awareness of their patterns and behaviour.
- Recognises their stories.
- Is okay with being misunderstood and doesn't need to defend itself.
- Can let go of old resentments and grievances.
- Recognises that multiple realities can co-exist.
- Recognises that different opinions can help us grow.
- Feels comfortable in own skin.
- Feels no need to judge others or self.
- Has nothing to prove.
- Responds rather than reacts.
- Is open to considering new experiences, ideas, worldviews.
- Is able to observe the ego.
- Is able to self-regulate during challenges.

Practice

It's time to get real. Take a look at the previous list of Ego Self traits. Circle the points that you think you have a tendency towards. This practice is going to take some serious honesty, and may expose some of our shadow. But that's what we're here for!

Remember, emerging in awareness is usually a process rather than an instant occurrence. Maybe you still fight with your spouse, but you nip it in the bud before either of you flood with emotion. Or you're snappy with your mother, but you recognise it and apologise for your tone. Perhaps you notice a pattern *after* you've already repeated it. It's important to recognise that you will still experience overwhelm, be defensive, take things personally and find yourself triggered by the people in your life. However, the very act of spotting it is the practice of healing. The greatest damage is done while unconscious. So, celebrate your wins, even if your win is simply having noticed your own unconsciousness. Because every time you recognise your unconsciousness, you are, in fact, strengthening your consciousness.

Being self-aware and prepared to question your thoughts and actions makes you a safer person for your loved ones. They'll know you're prepared to reflect rather than hold tight for the ego's sake.

Can you remember a time when you were experiencing conflict or challenge, but were able to bring your conscious self to the table? How did this change the interaction?

You'll know you're emerging from the grip of the ego when you notice your reactivity has lessened or disappeared. Very slowly, the over-sensitive ego is learning how to relax. We are beginning to relate from the core of our authentic self, from our essence.

Tip

Saying, 'This is who I am, like it or leave it,' can hinder our relationship potential. We need to be willing to consider where we can grow and evolve. If your loved one approaches you with feedback or a request to change, before you react, let the ego soften and consider if there's any truth to what they are saying. When we bring a growth mentality to our connections, we recognise that traits are not fixed and a relationship is an ever-evolving entity. Most of us never learnt how to communicate and navigate the road of relating. This, like any skill, can be cultivated to make the path smoother.

1: UNDERSTANDING HUMANS

Detouring
Conflict

Make yours a peaceful journey

2

In order to survive, we need food and water. A relationship also needs key basic elements to survive and thrive. Unfortunately, most of our relationships are starving, and we don't realise how readily available abundance is to us.

We're about to uncover simple yet powerful ideas and practices that will have your connections full to the brim. When we're feeling full, we have less to fight about. These ideas aren't complicated, nor will they take a lot of your time. By making small adjustments to the way we relate, we can completely change the health of our relationships. We just need to know how.

Be intentional

Nothing happens without intention. Until we bring awareness to our unconscious behaviour, we will assume that's 'just how things are' or 'just how our dynamic is'. By bringing intention to our actions, we have the ability to change the quality of our experience. So it's imperative we are intentional in our relationships; that we consciously make a decision to invest by actively working on our connections.

The healthiest relationships come from consciously nurtured connections. Think of it like caring for a plant, and ensuring that it gets enough sunlight and water. We can nourish our relationships in a similar way, by providing the elements that keep them healthy. The most important moments in our relationships will rarely look like fireworks or grand gestures. While these are wonderful ways to create shared narratives, it's in the everyday effort that emotional connectivity best blooms. Love and meaning is cumulative, cultivated during the seemingly mundane, everyday moments. It's important inner work, and isn't reliant on the validation or input of outside factors.

Practice

Let's inject some intent. Think of a relationship in your life you'd like to improve. We'll be referring to this connection as your 'chosen person'. As we move through the chapter, I'll be asking you questions and giving you homework to actively apply to this interaction. You're about to discover first-hand how the tools work!

Want to take this practice one step further? Involve the person you're thinking of. Make a commitment to work on your connection by doing the practices from this chapter together.

Get to know your loved ones

The better you know the people in your life, the more you'll understand their behaviour. If you can recognise their insecurities, fight styles, triggers, patterns, needs and desires, you'll know what to look out for. You'll take tricky moments less personally, be able to see conflict looming and be better equipped to handle the lows. You'll understand their perspective, and know how to support their dreams and help them feel loved.

Get familiar with your family and friends by asking important questions and listening to the way they express their needs. Regular interactions and quality time will help you build a solid friendship that offers a foundation to weather conflict.

Tip

Applying the tools from my book *How to Have Meaningful Relationships* will offer additional ways to get to know your loved ones on an empowering new level.

'Love and meaning is cumulative, cultivated during the seemingly mundane, everyday moments.'

LOVE LANGUAGE

Feeling loved is one of our greatest human needs, but for various reasons, we often don't feel loved by our loved ones, and vice versa. The reality is almost always that our loved ones *do* love us, but they often don't know how to express it, or aren't conscious of the importance of doing so.

In his renowned book *The Five Love Languages*, Dr Gary Chapman teaches how, as individuals, we express and receive love in different ways. He calls these our love languages.

Dr Chapman outlines five different languages in which people give and receive love: Words of Affirmation, Acts of Service, Receiving Gifts, Quality Time and Physical Touch. If you and your loved one express your love in different ways, it can feel like you're speaking two different languages. You're not going to understand each other.

If feeling loved is imperative yet we are not registering the way our loved one is expressing their love, major cracks begin to appear in our relationship. When we don't feel loved, we may seek to have our needs met in other, often detrimental, ways. We might use nagging, harsh words and criticism to get what we want. The sad thing is, often our loved ones *do* love us and *are* showing us that love, but if your love language is different, you may not be able to recognise it.

When you have the ability to identify someone's love language, you open up a beautiful new understanding of them – and you let their love in. This might be a parent helping you mend something at your home (Acts of Service), your sister wanting to take you to a gig or on a picnic (Quality Time), or a friend giving you a compliment about your work (Words of Affirmation). You learn to become multilingual in the languages of your loved ones. By observing a loved one's words and behaviour, you can pick their love language – and then speak it with them. Imagine how much this can fill them up, because they feel seen and heard – and in turn fill you up, because you can show how much you care about them. You're bringing ease, flow and harmony to the connection.

Feeling fully loved and giving love can ease what previously felt like unsolvable problems. Dr Chapman uses the analogy of each of us having a love tank. Speaking someone's love language, and doing so regularly, fills up their tank. When someone feels filled with love, rarely will they feel the need to find faults and focus on the negative.

Practice

- Identify the primary way you give and receive love. What fills you up? Is it when someone goes out of their way to help you? Or when you receive a loving compliment? Perhaps you feel cared for when a loved one gives you a thoughtful gift. Or when they carve out time to spend with you. Maybe you feel most loved when you receive that much-needed hug. If you're not sure what your love language is, take a look at the quiz on Dr Chapman's website, which may help you recognise it.

- What do you think your chosen person's love language is? How do they consistently reach out to you with loving gestures? You'll find clues in their behaviour, words, and also the things they complain about.

- Have a conversation with your chosen person about love languages. Ask them to guess theirs, and let them know which is yours. Now, come up with a game plan about how you can best speak each other's language.

- Commit to expressing love through your chosen person's love language on a daily basis, or each time you see them. Intentionally make the expression of love a part of your regular relationship encounters.

TRIGGERS

A trigger is a flashback. It's where you experience an emotional response to something in the present that reminds you of a previous trauma or core wound. Graphic images can trigger some people, for example, while more subtle songs and smells may be triggering for others. Or perhaps you might be triggered by someone speaking over you, leaving you feeling unheard, or by an argument with a partner, making you worried they'll end the relationship.

A trigger sets off alarm bells in your system, telling you you're in danger and that you need to protect yourself. Usually, you're not conscious of what the situation is reminding you of; it's a physiological reaction beyond cognitive thought. That reaction may be extreme, because your system is flooded with emotion and may automatically revert to fight or flight mode.

There's no need to judge our triggers or those of our loved ones. Instead, just become aware of them. They're another piece of our personal puzzle – and a part we can learn to understand and work with. Learning our loved ones' triggers allows us to be sensitive to them and understand when and why they get activated. Sharing our triggers with our loved ones can elevate our relationships to a more meaningful plane. There's something very special about doing this – it's incredibly intimate, and requires deep trust.

Why? Because you're essentially exposing your jugular. When someone knows your deepest sensitivities, they have the power to hurt you more than anyone else. But if treated with care, triggers can act as a gateway to knowing each other more deeply, allowing us to become aware of the issues that have shaped us. It opens up a context to offer understanding, rather than judgement.

If we aren't sensitive to the triggers of our loved ones, we will not only set them off, but we may also lack sensitivity when they respond in a way that we perceive as unfair or over the top. We won't understand why they are doing what they are doing. For those of us being triggered, we may respond with anger, fear and pain, and project unfairly onto our loved ones.

It's important to note that just because something is a trigger doesn't mean it has to stay that way. Healing can happen as we create new experiences and associate new meaning with situations. It takes time, but it's certainly possible to release some of our triggers within the safety of a loving relationship, where the other person's grace enables us to explore why we do what we do. As we become more aware of our triggers, we start to witness our feelings and create space between the trigger and the reaction. Each time we observe it, we slowly begin to release it.

Practice

Be curious about your loved ones and their histories. Understanding their past is an important step towards loving more skilfully.

Begin by paying attention to the situations that upset them most. Have you noticed similar patterns in your arguments with loved ones? Do you or your loved ones react in seemingly extreme ways to a particular situation or behaviour?

'Intentionally make the expression of love a part of your regular relationship encounters.'

EXPLORING TRIGGERS

Here are some common sensitivities you could gently delve into with your chosen person:

- Did they lose a parent or a sibling?
- Were they bullied or socially excluded?
- Were their parents overprotective, unaffectionate, emotionally unavailable, or dominating?
- Were they neglected or abused?
- What was their family dynamic around money?
- Did they feel that they were being compared to a sibling or other children?
- Did they feel like they weren't a priority?
- How were they labelled as a child?
- Did they have unrealistic expectations or unnecessary pressure placed upon them?
- Did they have a parent who abused substances?
- Did they have a parent or sibling who was unwell?
- What was their parents relationship like?
- What happened in their past intimate relationships?

In intimate relationships, it can also be helpful to honestly ask yourself, 'Are there similarities between my partner's parents and me?' The parent/child relationship is often the most sensitive source for triggers. So if you have traits or behaviours that remind your partner of their parents, they are more likely to be upset by those behaviours.

Practice

Take a look at the list on the previous page and think about where your own sensitivities and triggers may lie. Start by simply answering each question. You may find that, as you consider your history, you begin to link your past experiences with your current behaviours, exposing the 'Why' behind your reactions. Once you know, you can begin to articulate this to your loved one in a time of peace and calm. As we continue to navigate our vulnerabilities, we move closer to harmony by minimising the negative impact they have on those we care most about.

Next, it's time to observe. When you're feeling triggered, take a moment, pause and ask yourself: 'What is this situation reminding me of?' You may notice a memory resurface.

This is a helpful tool for your relationships, too. If a loved one has a sudden reaction, you might recognise their old wounds resurfacing. While it's never an excuse for them to treat you badly, you can compassionately observe the reasons behind their responses. It's personal for them, so you know not to take it personally.

Tip

Remember that even the happiest, healthiest, most
super-conscious people still have things that aggravate
or provoke them. What's important is that you know
what those things are, both for you and your loved ones,
so you can respond with awareness when they come up.

MANAGE YOUR EXPECTATIONS

No one person can give you everything you need. Our
relationships go awry when we focus on an ideal we've
created of how our loved ones should behave and what
they should do for us. Although this book looks at ways we
can improve our relationships, it's also important to take
the pressure off them. Be careful not to expect everything
from the one person, or ask them to meet unrealistic
standards of relational perfection. In our intimate
relationships, or in very close friendships, there can be an
expectation that the other is all we need. As a result, we
can ask our loved ones to wear many hats they may not
be suited to. When they don't fulfil our expectations, we
can feel let down. This would perhaps be less of an issue
if we lived in closer communities or tribes, with multiple
people fulfilling multiple roles for us. These days, we may
expect one person to be our best friend, lover, therapist,
provider, house cleaner, intellectual sparring partner and

master chef. We want them to make us laugh, be there when we cry, understand our innermost workings and be emotionally available to us at all times. Of course, this is only enhanced (and possibly caused) by media reinforcing the idea that 'real love' is an all-consuming experience; that we should be each others' everything in every waking moment!

It's important to have grace for our loved ones and let go of unrealistic standards that are impossible or unfair. It's important to recognise that their job was never to 'complete' us.

Although avoiding complacency is important, working on the relationship doesn't always need to feel like hard work. Lightening up and letting go of over-analysis and pressure can set your relationships moving in the very direction they need.

Unrealistic expectations might sound like this:

- This person should 'just know' what I need.
- This person should 'get' how I feel.
- This person should make me happy.
- This person shouldn't invest time in interests and friendships that don't include me.
- This person should tell me their most intimate secrets.
- This person should place my needs before their own.
- This person should always want to be physically intimate with me.
- This person should be close to my friends and family.
- This person should want to do the things I like to do.
- This person should unconditionally support my views and values.

Practice

Look at the above list. Are you placing unrealistic expectations or pressure on your relationship with your chosen person?

Are you placing unrealistic expectations or pressure on any of your other relationships?

ACCEPT YOUR DIFFERENCES

▼

There is no one person who is perfect for you. There's no such thing as 'your other half', and a 'be more like me' mentality will kill your connections. Our differences are what make us human. We come with different stories, personalities, triggers and goals. This offers some serious opportunities for incompatibility. Surrendering the need for sameness – in our ideas, interests, perspectives and opinions – is a major step towards harmony. We're not all meant to be the same. Some of our points of contention will always be there and may never be, or should never have to be, resolved. Let's start to understand – and then celebrate – our differences.

For example, one partner likes to move through life at a pretty relaxed pace. The other is more of a doer. How this plays out is one person may see something they think needs doing, and their partner doesn't get to doing it until months later, when they spontaneously feel the time is right. Frustrating for the doer? Yes. Different to them? Absolutely. Now, the doer could spend their time and energy pushing their partner to act differently, or begging them to change. They could fight about it. Or the doer could accept this is who their partner is, and they can negotiate how to work with their differences. Not only that, they could find benefits. For example, if they were both doers, they'd probably never stop. And if both of them were cruisers, there's a lot that wouldn't get done. The cruiser has taught the doer to carve out slabs of free time, and the doer is the firecracker that helps get the cruiser moving.

It's not your job to micro-manage your loved ones, but it is your job to create as much space as possible for them to be them, with all their idiosyncrasies. The differences we experience with our close connections aren't just in the way we do things, but also in the values we hold. Rather than pushing our opposing views onto someone, we can find other common ground to connect on. For example, I've made a lot of choices in my life that are in opposition to my father's beliefs. I continue to live in a way that doesn't always align with his worldview. Yet we have a beautiful, love-filled relationship, because we relate from an 'agree to disagree' space. We don't antagonise one another by trying to push our own views.

It's understandable that differences can and will create conflict. But if we can soften rather than harden, and accept that we can't control who people are, we create room to navigate new dynamics that hold each other's differences, and even allow them to benefit both parties. Knowing and accepting there are some things we can't change (and shouldn't try to) is empowering. So long as it doesn't require you to self-abandon, be prepared to work with their quirks and traits, and your varying histories. Rather than going around in endless circles on one issue, seek out ways to live harmoniously with your differences. Together, you're doing the important dance of diversity.

NOTE: There will be some differences in our relationships that we can't accept. These are the deal breakers that ultimately make us draw the line. The suggestions here are not to be applied in situations that are abusive and/or truly intolerable.

How does your personality differ to your chosen person's? How do they do things differently to you?

What does that teach you to cultivate within yourself?

How do your opinions differ to your chosen person's?

Can you accept that they have every right to that opinion, even if it's different to yours?

What opinions do you share? Where do you have common ground?

BE GENEROUS

Always lean in the direction of generosity, consciously seeking ways to fill up your people. Generosity goes beyond (but also includes) the idea of footing the bill. It's about loving abundantly, emotionally, energetically. When we do this in our relationships we create a culture of generosity – the other person feels safe to be generous back.

Below are some ways to be generous.

Appreciation

If you consistently show appreciation for who your loved ones are and what they do, your relationships will transform. Focus on what they *are* doing well. Recognise what *is* wonderful about them. Take note of the things you're grateful for, and let them know you're grateful. Much conflict occurs when someone doesn't feel seen or heard. When you appreciate who they are and what they do, you'll eliminate a whole heap of dissonance.

Do you acknowledge the small gestures your chosen person does for you?

Do you express gratitude when your chosen person does larger gestures for you?

Do you acknowledge the personality traits and characteristics you appreciate in your chosen person?

Tip

Humans are highly motivated by appreciation. The more gratitude you give for what you have, the more of it you'll experience down the track. We amplify what we focus on.

Practice

For the following fortnight, offer your chosen person verbal appreciation every day. Mark it in your calendar and tick it off. Tell them what you appreciate in their actions and their personality traits, without having any expectation that they will reciprocate. Observe how your dynamic shifts – because it will. I can honestly say this is one of the most powerful relationship tips I have. It WORKS.

'The roots of all goodness lie in the soil of appreciation for goodness.'

Dalai Lama

AVAILABILITY

Being available to build your relationship is imperative for a thriving connection. Distance and lack of contact can create a gap, which is often filled with disconnect and miscommunication.

Are you accessible and available for your chosen person? Can they catch you easily, or do they have to work hard to be with you?

NOTE: You can't be available to everyone at all times. You may need to identify the relationships you can offer your time to and those you can't. Communicate your availability clearly so they don't feel shunted if you're unable to show up.

ENGAGEMENT

When we are in the presence of our loved ones and they seek connection – in both the small and larger gestures – it's vital that we respond with genuine interest and emotional availability.
How do we do this?

● Listen to what they're saying. Be right there with them.

- Respond with presence to their attempts to connect – both big and small.
- Look into their eyes when they speak – which might mean putting down your phone.
- Be generous with their ideas, observations and opinions. You don't need to shut them down if they think differently to you.
- Allow multiple realities to exist – there's nothing wrong with having different opinions. Hear theirs, and state yours kindly.

When you're with your chosen person, are you present and engaged?

Do you shut them down unnecessarily?

When they are speaking, are you:

a. thinking about what you're going to say next?
b. looking at a screen or out the window?
c. offering them half-hearted or unenthusiastic acknowledgement?
d. looking in their eyes, offering open body language, giving a generous or kind-hearted response?

KINDNESS

When kindness is built into a relationship, you look out for each other. When someone knows you've got them, they are likely to be there for you, too. When this is established, we don't need to fight for what we want and need, because we're already on each other's side.

Wherever you can, back your chosen person's dreams, support their desires, meet their needs and go gently with their insecurities. Be compassionate and considerate.

When your chosen person expresses a desire or need, do you seek ways to support them?

Are you kind with your language and tone?

When you have different desires to your chosen person, do you seek a way to compromise?

SECURITY

What we're aiming for in healthy connections is a deep sense of security. The more secure someone feels in a connection, the less likely they are to seek attention and energy in detrimental ways. Don't hold back on letting your loved ones feel absolutely assured about where they stand with you.

Do you offer your chosen person a sense of security in your relationship, assuring them of where they stand?

Do you ever play games to make them feel insecure?

Do you know their love language?

Are you showing them secure love regularly?

NOURISH YOURSELF

One of the most generous things we can do in our relationships is take care of ourselves. After exploring the ways we can be generous in our connections, it may seem a little counterintuitive to take time and care for ourselves. But when we continually sacrifice our own needs, we start to draw on reserves we don't have to give, and this can wear us thin. We can become snappy, snarky, depressed and scattered. Not very generous. When this happens, we may find that no-one gets the best version of us anyway and, eventually, we may resent the people we're giving to. Pulling back is imperative if we are running so low we have nothing to give.

Part of this will be identifying what you need to nourish you, then offering what you can. You'll find when you're feeling full, you'll be overflowing with goodness to give. And your giving will come from joy rather than obligation, which will be far nicer to receive.

When we pull back in order to take care, this can sometimes be confronting for the ones we love, so be sure to reassure them when you're taking your space for you. Be clear in the way you communicate what you're doing and why.

NOTE: Be self-aware enough to identify the fine line between self-love and self-indulgence. Don't use this as an excuse to avoid responsibility or generosity. It can take a little time to find the line between the two, but eventually taking care will become second nature, with your giving coming from a healthy wellspring.

NOTE: Next time you are feeling irritable, resentful or pissed off with a loved one, ask yourself: 'Am I feeling nourished? Have I been practising self-care? Have I been meeting my needs?' Take a moment to check in on whether you are projecting from a place of lack. If so, be sure to take action to fill your cup.

Tip

Not only is it imperative to take care of our personal needs, it's also vital to communicate our relational needs ahead of time. Many fights could be avoided if we were simply honest about what we need rather than complaining about what we're not receiving.

2: DETOURING CONFLICT

Glennon Doyle

'If you
avoid the
conflict to
keep the
peace you
start a
war inside
yourself.'

Practice

Make it your aim to do something for yourself every day, just for you. At the end of each day, look back and see where you carved out space and time to nourish yourself and take care of your wellbeing.

BE COMMITTED

In a culture where it is easy to upgrade, swipe right and move on, we have a tendency to run when things get tough. One big fight and we're ready to walk away. One tricky phase and we're ready to call it quits.

When you establish a mentality that you are all in, conflict and fights feel a little less definitive. They are a darker-hued moment on a colourful journey. When we have a culture of commitment, we feel safe approaching the tough issues and uncomfortable conversations, and secure enough to raise our difficulties and concerns.

Addressing those things when they're small will prevent bigger conflict disasters down the track. So be sure to commit to addressing the challenges, to having the hard conversations, to enduring the tough times and to the relationship itself. If you have concerns, raise them. It's about mining for gold in the place we're in, rather than chasing after the next shiny gem.

Are you committed to your chosen person?

If yes, do you let them know and feel your commitment?

Do you have a tendency to run (or threaten to) when things get tough?

We are likely to continue to experience the same challenges, patterns and confrontations in our connections until we learn the lesson and identify where the patterns are coming from. As Pema Chodron says, 'Nothing ever goes away until it teaches us what we need to know.' So before you bail, take a good look at the situation and ask yourself: 'What is the lesson here? What is this teaching me about myself? What are my patterns?'

I am not suggesting you stay in a relationship that is abusive, toxic or doesn't feel right for you. The intention here is that we commit first and foremost to ourselves. Sometimes that means leaving, and then doing the work to ensure we don't repeat the same patterns again. More on that in Chapter 8.

SOFTEN

We live in a culture that supports striving, fighting, having an edge and winning your battles. These qualities can have us kicking goals in our career or hobbies and protecting us where we need it. However, if we bring this attitude into our relationships, we can constantly feel on edge or be overly reactive.

Sometimes what we consider to be our strength is the very thing that's getting in the way of a connected, intimate relationship. When we soften, we learn to become emotionally flexible. We can flow, adapt, drop our barriers and let love in. Rather than being hypervigilant and looking for a fight, we can be vulnerable and present.

Many of us equate softness with being a walkover, but you don't need to let go of your boundaries or self-respect. It's about quieting the part of you that's constantly ready to defend, argue or 'win'. It also means trusting your relationships and the intentions of your loved ones that little bit more. When you soften your heart, you're not afraid to show your vulnerabilities or express your love. You open up to possibilities and surrender that fixed mindset. Softening is often the hardest move of all.

Practice

Think about your relationship with your chosen person. What would be a vulnerable move for you? Is there a part of you that would be a challenge to express or reveal? Take a tiny step towards softening in your connection. That might mean changing your normal responses or expressing something you normally wouldn't say. Be sure to pat yourself on the back afterwards – this takes a lot of strength and courage!

Practice

Consider the role you take on most days. Does it require you to have an edge, to be hypervigilant, to compete or kick goals? If so, you may find it tricky to switch off from that mode, and you may be bringing that energy into your connections. Before you see your chosen person, make it a ritual to do something symbolic that represents a state change for yourself. Whether it's having a shower, changing your outfit or practising ten deep breaths, do something that helps you shift into a softer mode.

Practice

In the next challenging conversation you come up against, take note of a desire to defend yourself. Notice if your walls want to go up, and ask yourself: 'What would happen if I softened in this moment?'

CONSCIOUSLY CREATE YOUR HISTORY

Every event, interaction and conversation in your connections weaves together to create the fabric of your relationship history. So it's important to consciously create experiences in the present to become positive memories of the past. When you constructively build layers to your connection, you build a stronger base. When the tough times hit, we have a tendency to focus on the negative, but if we've built up a backlog of positive experiences, we have a foundation to rely on. We can know that care and love is there and we have something worth fighting for. Continue to create and recreate a beautiful world for the two of you that will see you through the tough times, and prevent them from occurring as often.

Practice

Create a ritual that connects you with
your chosen person on a regular basis.
This might be a weekly date or a monthly
wine night. Maybe it's a walk on a Tuesday
morning or a cup of tea together at the
end of the day. Creating shared rituals
helps us to create and maintain a feeling
of closeness.

'Continue to create and
recreate a beautiful
world for the two
of you.'

Practice

Create an experience or event that will become a standout memory in your relationship history. Get creative and map out something special for your chosen person. Getting out of the everyday routine and envisioning a special shared experience will add richness to your connection.

When we learn to understand the unique languages of our loved ones, we embark on our journey together towards harmony. While there will be conflict along the way, nurturing and nourishing your relationships is sure to make it a smoother ride.

By tending to our connections, we grow. Let's feed them the basic elements to help them thrive: generosity, appreciation, security. And weed out the toxic: unrealistic expectations, micro-managing and hypervigilance. These have no place in your garden.

Take your time to gently work through your exercises, then take a look around you. You're in bloom.

Confrontation without conflict

The
Lead-up

3

There will be times when confrontation is unavoidable. Sometimes the only option is to face the problem head-on. But head-on doesn't have to mean hostile. It's how you handle the confrontation that's important. To have a harmonious relationship isn't to have a challenge-free relationship. Rather, it's having the capacity to remain conscious enough in our connections that we create a culture of safety, where we are safe to disagree and then navigate our way through, minimising the damage and maximising the growth.

Understand what's happening physiologically

It's natural to view conflict as negative. Most of us haven't seen healthy conflict and reconciliation methods modelled, and have instead witnessed aggressive, passive-aggressive, destructive and nasty interactions. These kinds of interactions can do lasting damage – even if you're not the one in the firing line.

Because we are conditioned to perceive conflict as a negative or threatening experience, our nervous system becomes alerted at the first sign of a challenge. If conflict escalates (or feels like it's going to), our systems can go into high defence. This means we respond in either flight, fight, freeze (shutting down) or fawn (complying with someone to save yourself or avoid conflict) mode. None of these reactions are very helpful when resolving disagreements. When the body and mind are overwhelmed and under stress, it is impossible to think straight or communicate rationally. This is why conflict often ends up as an unresolved cycle – our physiology is on high alert, telling us we need to defend ourselves. While in this mode, it's very hard to convince our system to relax and see things clearly. Our nervous system is doing its job – to protect us – but often at a cost to our connection.

Understanding our physiology (and that of others) will open up a space for grace, help us take things less personally, and allow us to – over time – re-write our responses.

Practice

What's your most common response to conflict?

a. Flight
b. Fight
c. Freeze
d. Fawn

Now think about a loved one. What do you think is their most common response to conflict? Understanding that they are experiencing a physiological response may help you to widen your perspective and have some empathy for their reaction.

Practice discernment – if, when, how

DO I NEED TO RAISE THIS?

As we evolve in relational awareness, we begin to refine our reactivity. When an issue arises, the first question we ask is: Do I need to raise this?

We practice discernment when we look at the bigger picture, rather than hyperfocusing on the minor things. We ask: Can I let this go? Is this critical in the grand scheme? Is there something going on for them that means I need to apply grace? Is this a one-off incident or an ongoing issue?

And perhaps the most important question: Which action best serves us both? If you don't address the issue and that results in resentment down the track, you're not doing anyone any favours by holding it in. But if, with space, time and perspective, the issue is likely to genuinely dissolve or resolve itself, perhaps just let it go.

WHEN SHOULD I RAISE THIS?

There are plenty of times when it is not appropriate to raise an issue. Ignoring the timing of a sensitive subject can be the deciding factor in whether the conversation achieves resolution or heads south. Choosing our timing wisely requires us to be considerate of the circumstances.

Avoid raising the issue if you or the other person are:

- stressed
- tired
- frustrated
- in the middle of a project or activity
- in the middle of a crisis
- lacking time to find resolution in the moment
- in front of other people
- hungry

It's important to be selective with your timing, but it's equally important not to let things build up. If you're finding it difficult to find an ideal time, then book a date to talk. When you dedicate a specific time and place for your discussion, you are both more likely to be in a clear headspace for resolution. Give it priority, like you would for a work meeting.

HOW SHOULD I RAISE THIS?

If you go in guns blazing, your challenging conversation is going to get even more difficult. An aggressive approach is likely to put your loved one on high alert. They'll either step up to the power plate and face you head-on, or they'll retreat until they feel safe to return.

A big danger here is that you might end up arguing over the argument, rather than the original issue. Aggressive approaches are common, as are defensive reactions. But with work, we can start to change our style. Once you proceed with care and patience, you'll begin to see good results. You'll move forward with conflict resolution, and you may even find yourself looking forward to these difficult discussions. Growth feels good.

Tip

Change location. If you live together or work together, shift things up by stepping out. Getting outdoors can have a calming effect, so head for the backyard, park, or a wide open space. It can also help to walk or sit side by side while you have your discussion, as this feels less confrontational than facing each other head-on.

Find your centre

Create clarity and calmness by getting clear on your feelings *before* your conversation. Take time to process your thoughts and emotions in the way that works best for you. Some people find journalling helpful because the words physically leave their mind and land on the paper. Or you could practise the conversation aloud, into a voice recorder or with a therapist or trusted friend. You want to leave this process feeling confident that you know what you'd like to say.

Questions to ask yourself

Before you make the call, arrange the catch-up or start the conversation, it can be helpful to get really honest with yourself by asking:

- Am I prepared to consider their feelings?
- Can I express strong feelings in a kind way?
- Am I prepared to own my part?
- Am I prepared to be respectful?
- Do I have room for grace?

If the answer to *any* of these questions is 'no', you may not be ready to have this conversation. Sure, it may feel more authentic or even cathartic to speak your mind without filtering your feelings, but if that's going to put the other person on the defence – which is likely – they won't hear what you have to say.

Additionally, it's helpful to zoom out and ask yourself what your ultimate intention is within this relationship. Do I want reconciliation? Do I want an ongoing relationship with this person? Do I want to continue to experience conscious communication? Getting clear on your macro intention will deeply affect how you show up to the conversation, and this energy will then reverberate throughout the entire interaction.

State your intentions

Be clear from the outset that you're *seeking resolution* and not simply attacking the other person's character or wanting to go a couple of rounds. The following is an example of a line my husband uses that works really well for us: 'There's something I want to talk about, but I really don't want it to turn into a fight. Can we try our best to prevent that from happening?'

I will sometimes use: 'Can we have a conscious conversation about something I'm struggling with?'

These approaches give the other person's system a little warning that a potentially difficult discussion is about to happen.

NOTE: Even the hardest conversations can be had without name-calling, nasty one-liners or intimidating tones. When we emotionally mature in the way we relate, we recognise that we can be considerate and kind with our language while simultaneously feeling frustrated, angry, hurt or challenged.

USE 'I FEEL' STATEMENTS

Using 'I feel' statements is a golden communication technique which encourages bringing your needs into the conversation by beginning your statements with 'I'. This could be 'I feel ...' or 'I would like ...' This flips your statement so it's about you, not the other person. The idea here is that you communicate your perspective without blaming or shaming, meaning your loved one is less likely to feel cornered or defensive. It helps your conversation get off to the best start, and is much more constructive than using accusatory statements.

More golden direction comes from Gary Chapman, author of *The Five Love Languages*. He advises presenting your desires as requests, not demands. Instead of telling someone what they've done wrong, or what they should be doing, flip it into a request and watch how well it lands.

For example, here's an example of an accusatory statement: 'You never make me feel special. You always do fun things with your friends.'

And here's that statement flipped into a request: 'I love trying new things with you. Would you like to get away for a weekend together next month?'

Another helpful practice is to explain that you have a problem you'd like their help fixing, rather than telling them they are the problem and need to change.

So, rather than: 'What you said to me the other day

was horrible. I can't stop thinking about it. You should never speak to me like that again.'

Try: 'I have a problem I'm hoping you can help me fix. I'm feeling very hurt by a comment you made, and I can't seem to move on. Can you help me resolve this so I can sleep well tonight?'

Own your part

In the previous section, I suggested you ask yourself: 'Am I prepared to own my part?'

This is where I put you to the test. If you can take any responsibility for the situation in these early stages, you're in for a much easier conversation. The other person is less likely to feel attacked and more likely to follow suit. Let them know where you share some responsibility, and acknowledge how you contributed to the situation.

What if it doesn't work?

It won't always work. No matter how conscious you are, or how many of these approaches you try, there's always a chance your fix might escalate into a fight. Even with a gentle and caring approach, you won't always be able to spare their feelings. Some things are simply hard to receive.

It's important to stay level, without assigning blame to either side. Your job is not to control their reaction, but to manage your response to their reaction.

If things are headed downhill, try to lift them back up. Defuse the tension by empowering yourselves and seeing the positive. This could be a reminder of your good intentions, or a genuine compliment for your loved one. Showing them that you think highly of their character takes away the sting if they're feeling personally attacked, and calms their nervous system so they can hear you.

TRY SOMETHING LIKE: 'I'm sorry. I care about you and I don't want you to feel attacked. I want to talk about this because I love you and I'm hoping we can fix this. I'd really like to hear your perspective.'

Tip

The upcoming chapters will offer further insight into what we can do in the heat of an argument. But for now, dog-ear this chapter, so the next time a challenge arises you can easily find these pages. By walking yourself through these points before raising the issue at hand, you'll exponentially increase your chances of an early resolution.

Tip

Remind yourself that if conflict *does* arise, it doesn't have to be a disaster. Our goal isn't to reach some unrealistic intention of 100 per cent connection or permanent peace. As we'll discover throughout this book, our intention is to create safety in moments of disconnection and reduce the refractory period it takes to bounce back from them. Remember, conflict can be one of the greatest opportunities for personal growth and relational depth if we stay open and receptive to the lessons it can bring.

Uncovering the strategies

What's your *Fight style?*

4

So, you're fighting the fight. Maybe your guns are blazing, perhaps you're in denial, or you're turning the silent treatment up loud. These are examples of fight styles, and we all have our signature. Our fight style steps in during conflict to influence the other person. Essentially, we use it to dominate the conversation or control the situation. This is usually an unconscious process that can create an unhealthy way of relating.

When we understand our style, we can bring consciousness to our behaviour, and choose to shift into a healthier way of relating – and arguing.

When we recognise our loved one's fight style, we can use methods to shift them out of their cycle and encourage them to communicate from a healthier position. We are also less likely to be controlled by their techniques.

Witness awareness and radical self-honesty are the first steps to changing our habits and addressing our fight styles. By opening up to a higher state of self-awareness, we can pivot to a more positive place. Together, we can fight the good fight.

Fight styles

The Brawler

Hello, blazing guns. The Brawler has no fear of confrontation. They are ready for a fight, and often even enjoy it. Trademark traits include aggressive, intimidating and overpowering energy to escalate the exchange and control the other person. They need to win, often at all costs, and will use threatening, bullying and strong tones to be victorious.

The Brawler will often see opportunities for confrontation even when they don't exist, or jump on an opportunity as soon as it appears. They'll be ready to road-rage, blow up at a sales worker or get fiery at a family gathering. They are incredibly defensive and almost impossible to reason with. Brawlers are unlikely to own their actions, especially during a confrontation.

In more extreme cases, there can be a threat of violence when dealing with a Brawler. These types are more likely to do damage to themselves, others or the world around them during confrontation.

Communicating with a Brawler? Try this:

A Brawler is difficult to approach, and they won't hear your side of the story in the heat of the moment. They've got their boxing gloves on, fists raised and they're ready to fight. The bigger a scene they can make, the better.

They will need some time to storm it out, but the good news is, they run out of steam eventually. At that point, you'll be in a better position to rationalise with them.

In the meantime, do your best to avoid becoming defensive in the face of their accusations. They are fighting to be heard, wanting to express themselves and get their feelings on the table. Even if you don't agree with what they're saying, you can help defuse the intensity by seeing things from their perspective and letting them know you understand where they are coming from.

Try saying something like: 'I understand you feel ... because ...' You're not telling them they're right, you're letting them know you understand why they feel that way. This gives them less to fight for.

Be prepared to own your actions if you think they have a point. Just because they're coming on strong doesn't mean they're in the wrong. They might be upset or angry for good reason, so if you agree, apologise. The sooner you do this, the sooner the fight will end. Be sure your apology is genuine. Don't apologise just to appease them, or you'll feel resentful down the track.

If you're finding it hard to stay regulated, or you feel like your boundaries are being crossed, it can be helpful or necessary to remove yourself from the situation. Creating space can defuse the intensity, giving everyone time to calm down and get their nervous systems back into balance. We'll talk more about this in Chapter 5, and give you a method for doing this while ensuring the Brawler doesn't feel abandoned, ignored or more aggravated.

If you feel like you are being threatened, or you're concerned about your wellbeing, it's crucial to remove yourself from danger. In violent or abusive relationships the only option is to leave and seek shelter elsewhere.

Are you a Brawler? Try this:

Be honest: are you addicted to drama, getting off on a fight or seeking a hit of energy? Pause before approaching a situation and ask yourself the following questions:

- Am I prepared to be fair?
- Am I prepared to be kind?
- Can I use a gentle tone of voice?

If the answer is no, take time before you confront the other person. Do something active, like going for a run, to let off some steam. Wait until your system is calm before sending the text, making the call or addressing the other person.

What does the healthy version look like?

One of the great things about the Brawler is they aren't afraid to address issues, have uncomfortable conversations and explore challenges. A Brawler is bold, and that can be a real asset. Once they've learned to curb their fire, they can practise doing this in a conscious way to help avoid long-term damage and resentment in their relationships.

The Ostrich

Things are heating up? This head's going in the sand. The Ostrich will either pretend nothing is wrong, or they will people-please to bypass uncomfortable conversations. They are more concerned with avoiding conflict than they are with solving problems, and will minimise or make light of an issue rather than attempting to resolve it. Here's where you'll see the classic 'sweep it under the rug' technique. An Ostrich is all for out of sight, out of mind.

They often grew up in an environment where conflict was dangerous or didn't lead to positive outcomes, so for them, it feels safer to avoid it.

Unfortunately, this is a short-term solution for harmony. People-pleasing, saying yes when they mean no, or squelching their inner truth ultimately builds resentment. They are at risk of blowing up later, which reiterates their belief that conflict is unsafe. Alternatively, they may end a relationship with no notice and miss out on important opportunities to grow through challenges.

An Ostrich will find it hard to own their own actions. Rather than admitting to themselves that they need to apologise, they'll avoid someone, or act as though everything is fine and carry on pretending nothing has happened.

Communicating with an Ostrich? Try this:

We need to go gently with an Ostrich. They will run at the first sign of a fight, so be clear that your intention is for resolution, and that you don't intend to be confrontational. Reassure them that they are safe to speak truthfully, and affirm them when they do.

Be ready to receive what they have to say with an open mind. This will create a new story for them around what it means to have challenging conversations, and will show them that it is safe to do so. This is something that can take time and repeated experiences for them to learn.

Are you an Ostrich? Try this:

Let's begin with some staying power. Instead of leaving at the first sign of trouble, make a conscious decision to stay and work through the issue. Be honest and vulnerable about how hard this is for you. You may say, 'It's really hard for me to have this conversation. I'm scared it will turn into a fight. Can we try to go gently with each other?' or 'I have a fear of confrontation that makes me avoid difficult conversations. Can we try to be kind to each other in this conversation?'

If it feels safer to avoid an exchange, or you recognise you've put your head in the sand, it's not too late to revisit the discussion once the intensity of the moment has passed. Again, choose to share vulnerably, such as, 'I avoided saying this earlier, because I didn't know how to express myself. Can I share with you now how I feel?'

When you learn how to identify your needs and recognise your inner truth, you can flourish. In everyday situations, start asking yourself: 'Is this true for me?' It can be as simple as deciding where to go for dinner, or which movie to watch. Start asserting your opinions in the small moments and you'll begin learning how to express yourself in the tougher times.

What does the healthy version look like?

One of the wonderful things about an Ostrich is that once they learn to express themselves, they are often collaborative, respectful in their disagreements, and looking for win-win solutions. Additionally, there are times when it genuinely makes sense to avoid conflict. Ostriches have the ability to choose their timing well because unlike the Brawler, they can wait to get something off their chest.

The Victim

The Victim incites guilt and pity to gain energy and control in a fight. They either make you feel sympathy for them, or they make you feel responsible for their pain.

A Victim will focus on their hardships, and how they have been wronged. They are often disappointed in people and feel like they are constantly being let down. In an argument, they will want to show how they are being wronged, pained and hurt.

Communicating with a Victim? Try this:

The Victim is desperate to be felt and heard. Acknowledging them is the most effective way to communicate. If you try to minimise their hurt, ignore it or explain it away they are likely to keep pushing their point or escalate their expression of pain, which means the story or experience becomes even more embedded. When you acknowledge a victim's pain, they are less likely to need to show it. Some will even flip their attitude and say something like, 'Oh it's not that bad after all.'

Before we go on, it's important to note that just because someone shows emotion, cries, gets upset or shares vulnerably *does not automatically mean they are 'playing the victim'*. It would be detrimental to make that assumption and disregard their very real and valid feelings. Take a moment to ask yourself honestly if you have let them down, or if there is truth to what they are saying. They might be upset for good reason. If you agree they have a point, be prepared to apologise. The sooner you do this, the sooner you will find resolution. However, remember that just because someone places responsibility on you doesn't mean you have to accept that responsibility. It is up to you to decide how much you can personally offer in any relationship, and it's important to communicate that clearly. For example, 'I understand you were hurt that I wasn't available to talk to you the other day. I want to support you, but I am unable to speak on the phone during work hours.' And then outline what you *can* offer, and how you can show up.

How can we decipher the difference between genuine pain and someone playing the Victim? If someone is stuck in a Victim role, they'll continue to pull more energy from you even after you've acknowledged them or apologised. So if the guilt trips keep coming, new accusations appear and they continue to behave as though they've been hard done by, they may be trying to control you with their pain. Also take note of what they are like in everyday life. Is constantly complaining about life their default behaviour? Are your regular conversations with them often tinged with their hardships? If this is the case, it's more likely this is their fight style. If they are generally a positive person, it's possible they are simply having a vulnerable moment.

If you genuinely feel they are playing the Victim, state how you feel to help them see that you're not buying into it. 'I feel like you're trying to control me by making me feel guilty.' If this is genuinely how you feel, acknowledge what is going on and be clear on your boundaries. You can let them know you still want to show up and care for them (if this is true for you) in the capacity that is possible for you.

Are you a Victim? Try this:

Asking for what you need is going to be a gamechanger for you. Clearly communicate ahead of time how someone can best support you. Give the other person the greatest chance they have to help you. Victims have a tendency to get upset at someone for not providing something that they never clearly asked for, or that they wanted within an impossible timeframe. This allows the Victim to reinforce their story of being hard done by.

Victims can sometimes be like the boy who cried wolf. By lamenting as a way to gain attention, they can gain a reputation for doing so, which can lead to them being dismissed when they truly need help. Again, this reinforces the story of being a Victim.

To grow in consciousness, it's vital you are completely honest with yourself. Recognise where you are addicted to your pain cycles and acknowledge the games you're playing to gain energy and attention from others. It's important to learn how to fill your own cup, stand on your own feet and become capable. You will feel far more empowered. People will want to be there for you when you are no longer trying to suck energy from them. They'll also recognise that when you do make requests or express your hurt, you are being genuine.

What does the healthy version look like?

A huge positive of the Victim is that they are able to share vulnerably. Vulnerability is an absolute superpower. This can open up a space for real feelings to be expressed on both sides. When they become aware of their tendencies, Victims are less likely to get caught up in their 'stories' because they know that just affirms the reality of their pain. Instead, they are able to clearly state where they are hurting, or where things have been painful. Then they can encourage the other side to do the same.

The Ice Queen/King

This frosty reception ain't so chill. The Ice Queen/King freezes people out, gives the silent treatment and is distant to the point of almost disappearing. They'll avoid engaging in discussion, cooperating or working towards a solution. A huge giveaway: saying 'I'm fine' when it's clear they mean the opposite. Rather than directly saying what they are upset about, they will punish the other person with frosty silence.

By refusing to communicate, the Ice Queen/King controls the exchange by drawing it out, preventing the other person from finding solutions to address the conflict. It's a way of gaining power while appearing to be doing nothing.

This style can be a form of punishment for something that was said or done, or a roundabout way of communicating that something is wrong, while placing an expectation on the other person to know what it is. The Ice Queen/King often expects the information to be teased out of them, and will leave it up to the other person to work out how to do that.

The difference between an Ice Queen/King and an Ostrich is that although neither are communicating directly, the Ostrich will try to smooth things over or fake niceties, whereas the Ice Queen/King doesn't mind the distance, and uses it as a form of punishment and control.

NOTE: There is a difference between someone who is engaging in Ice Queen/King behaviour and someone who has genuinely shut down because they're feeling psychologically overwhelmed by a situation. There will be times when the threat of conflict feels so confronting that a person will disengage in order to cope. This is a physiological reaction based on survival psychology, as opposed to a conscious decision to control or punish the other person.

Communicating with an Ice Queen/King? Try this:

The person on the receiving end of this behaviour may feel hopeless, as though they have no control. Often they'll attempt their own passive-aggressive behaviour or silent treatment to cope. Alternatively, they may escalate their attempts to reach the other person, and may even become aggressive because they don't feel heard. This will give the Ice Queen/King even more reason to shut them out.

This fight style can be a result of growing up with people who didn't say what they were thinking, or where doing so had negative outcomes. As a result, the Ice Queen/King can genuinely find it difficult to open up and express themselves. Try to keep this in mind and be understanding when dealing with an Ice Queen/King. Even though it is infuriating and painful to be treated like this, lashing out or being frosty yourself will only drive a greater wedge between you.

Your ego will desperately want to play into the game. Here's where we feel the squeeze and use what we've learnt to rise above it. Once you recognise they are playing out their fight style, stay calm and avoid becoming defensive. Try to be gentle, rather than pressuring. Don't try to force them into opening up – give them the option to communicate, and let them know your intention is reconciliation. By being non-confrontational and loving, we relieve the pressure to continue the game. There's less motivation to keep trying to manipulate someone who is not engaging in the drama. You may choose to say something such as: 'I'd love for us to fix this problem. I'm here when you're ready' or 'I'd love to hear your point of view'. This opens up an invitation for discussion, while not pushing them to speak.

They may not initially reply in the way you would like – and don't expect an immediate response. You may need to gently extend the invitation again later. By staying calm and showing them you are not playing the game, they are more likely to break the cycle of their fight style. If this is a learnt behaviour from childhood, they may need to experience a number of occasions where communicating directly brings healthy outcomes.

This fight style is particularly painful for those with a fear of abandonment. Here, name your fears and feelings out loud: 'I feel afraid when you are silent towards me, like you don't consider me.' If you don't feel safe to do this with the person who is freezing you out, it can be incredibly helpful to talk to a professional.

Are you an Ice Queen/King? Try this:

You may not realise the extent of the pain you could be causing someone by freezing them out. It's possible your parents modelled this behaviour, so you think it's normal. To experience a healthier way of relating, you need to first acknowledge your actions. Notice when you begin to withdraw and challenge yourself to reach out. Respond to their attempts of connection. This may mean going against your conditioning, so your ego will certainly feel the squeeze. It may also feel quite vulnerable to lean into communicating when every part of you wants to freeze up. But it will feel good to thaw out.

What does the healthy version look like?

A beautiful asset of an Ice Queen/King is their comfort with – and encouragement of – breathing room. There are times when a situation can genuinely benefit from some space, for both parties to gain perspective and calm down. When Ice Queens/Kings bring awareness to their behaviour, they can instigate space, but do so consciously. Rather than stay in a situation that is escalating out of control, they can give it room to breathe, allowing time for perspective.

The Assassin

No go, low blow. The Assassin strikes below the belt, fights dirty and gets nasty – fast. They know your soft spots and will hit you right where it hurts. Insults, put-downs, sarcasm and gaslighting are all trademarks of an argument with an Assassin.

The Assassin can undermine another person's reality by denying facts or their feelings. They may attempt to convince the other person that they are imagining or making up their experience. They may deliberately use intimate information they have of others' deepest vulnerabilities to gain an advantage during an argument.

When they feel like they're losing a fight or being exposed, they will intentionally derail the conversation. This is a signature move for the Assassin. Rather than sticking to the situation at hand, they bring up new accusations and challenge the other person, often using insulting language to drive home their point.

They will point out the other person's personality flaws, rather than sticking to the initial issue, in an attempt to make the other person feel unworthy to respond. As a result, the receiver will either have to start defending themselves or may feel too inadequate to have a say in the matter.

In more extreme cases, Assassins can be downright emotionally abusive. If you feel like you are being psychologically threatened or you're concerned about your mental wellbeing, it's crucial to remove yourself from danger.

Communicating with an Assassin? Try this:

Being on the receiving end of this fight style can be debilitating. Over time you may experience insecurity, anxiety and a loss of self-esteem. You may question your intuition, experience, reality and even sanity.

It's important to develop a healthy dose of self-love and confidence to help you stay strong and true to yourself when dealing with an Assassin. Essentially, they are trying to bring you down, so it's important you build inner strength and self-assurance to hold your own.

Assassins are intimidating. Handling the intimidation means staying in your power and remaining clear-headed in the face of their barrage. It can be helpful to imagine you have a loving shield around you, then picture their accusations and comments as tiny pellets bouncing off it.

Stay centred and calm when talking about your experience and be sure to use the self-regulation practices that we'll be learning about in Chapter 5. Assassins often lack empathy, so don't count on a vulnerable share to reach them. In more extreme cases, your emotion or pain is exactly what they want to see – it may even give them motivation to push you even further.

You are more likely to throw them off centre by remaining neutral, grounded, level-headed and not buying into the drama. They're being nasty and are trying to entice you into their game. Staying calm and kind in your communication style can thwart their attempts. By refusing to fight, you take the fight out of the situation.

Even if you think their accusations are unfounded, avoid trying to defend yourself, as this will often lead to more derailing and accusations. Keep it simple with a statement such as, 'I'm sorry to hear that's what you think of me'. Learn to be okay with being misunderstood. Trying to justify or defend your character just pulls you back in and takes your energy.

When they try to derail the conversation, say 'I'm open to hearing about that, but let's stay with the issue at hand. I think we've almost sorted this.'

You can also throw them off their game by reiterating your own sense of self-worth. Try a statement such as 'I can see that you disagree, however I feel confident I'm doing a really good job'. By staying strong in self-love, you're showing them that their attempts to bring you down aren't working.

Swiftly finding a solution to their problem can also wrap up the fighting. Try a neutral statement that offers a solution that is a win-win or compromise.

In saying that, don't be too optimistic about reasoning with the Assassin. Know when to call Time Out on the conversation or situation. The Assassin will be laser-focused on winning in the moment, and can be easier to communicate with after some space apart.

Are you an Assassin? Try this:

It's crucial you become self-aware, and are honest with yourself about your behaviour and its impact on the people around you. Making an argument personal, being nasty, criticising someone's opinions, disregarding them and slamming their personality is a form of emotional aggression. It's important to understand that scaring someone, putting them in a position where it's hard for them to respond, or pushing them over their edge doesn't mean you've won. You've simply silenced them.

Be brutally honest with yourself about these shadow traits. Ask yourself what your bigger truth is: Do you want this relationship to work? Do you want a win-win outcome? Do you care about this person?

Be open to things not being black and white. Assassins often feel 100 per cent sure of themselves (or the image they've created for themselves), and therefore justify fighting to the bitter end. It's time to understand that multiple realities exist and that there are grey areas in every interaction. It's important to consider where you may be wrong or imperfect.

What does the healthy version look like?

Underneath the intensity of an Assassin is an innate ability to understand another person's sensitivities, soft spots and vulnerabilities. Assassins have a knack for seeing to the core of the other. Although it takes a huge leap in consciousness, if they can learn to transmute this skill for good, and bring empathy to the discussion, they have a wonderful ability to see both sides and swiftly get to the core of the issue. Of all the fight styles, this personality is most able to see the true reasons and vulnerabilities behind why a person is really fighting, helping them address the real issue at hand.

The Conscious Communicator

Ahh, a breath of fresh awareness. The Conscious Communicator takes steps to move towards the healthy version of their tendencies. They are prepared to have difficult conversations and acknowledge uncomfortable situations, and they do this with a genuine intention for resolution.

The Conscious Communicator integrates kindness and awareness into these challenges and has empathy for the other person's position – even if they don't agree with their perspective. They recognise that multiple realities can simultaneously exist, and make an effort to listen and understand the other person's feelings. You'll still notice them debating and expressing their side, but they seek ways to solve the issue rather than focusing on winning the fight. They are conscious of their tone, delivery and the words they use – no nasty one-liners here. Rather, they go gently with the insecurities and triggers of the other person. If the situation goes sideways, they make attempts to make amends and repair the damage.

A Conscious Communicator has the skills to witness when they are having a physiological reaction. They can then adjust themselves with self-regulation techniques or by taking a break. They can negotiate, compromise and find win-win solutions. Owning their mistakes and apologising comes easily, because they can spot where their ego has come into play. Rather than getting caught up in the little things, they zoom out and look at the bigger picture. They stay open to love, even when they're hurting.

The Conscious Communicator genuinely wants the best for the other person. They consider the other's emotions as valid and, because this respect is felt, they spend less time fighting.

Practice

Take a look at the fight styles outlined in this chapter. Which do you think is your default?

Although you will likely identify your primary style, you may be a combination of more than one. We sometimes adopt different styles for different people in our lives, according to what we've figured out works best. For example, you may be a Victim for your partner, but become a Brawler when you're online.

It's also possible to switch between styles during a fight, especially if you're not getting the results you desire. For example, you might start out as a Victim but when you don't get sympathy, you shift into Ice Queen/King.

WHERE DID YOUR FIGHT STYLE COME FROM?

Included in the inheritance we receive from our caregivers is our emotional cues. Much of what we believe about challenges, conflict, communication, intimacy and reconciliation was likely absorbed when we were young. It can be interesting to reflect on what you witnessed, and how that shows up in the way you operate.

Have you adopted a similar pattern? Or perhaps you have adopted a pattern that perpetuates or copes with what you've experienced. For example, if you grew up with a Brawler, you may have become a Victim, in the hope that they will feel sorry for you and change their behaviour.

Understanding your family dynamics often offers epiphanies about why we do things, and why we believe things need to be done a certain way. Some of these may be healthy and some may need to be upgraded. For example, we might reflect on how we felt when those fight styles were used on us, particularly if they were toxic.

Consider if you need to upgrade the model you learned. Most people do. To move forward, we need to separate our beliefs from what we've been modelled, and to develop our own ways to best relate and function within relationships.

If you had to guess, which fight style would your parents be?

In intimate partnerships the combination of your fight styles can really determine the flavour of your relationship. For example, two Brawlers may fight incessantly. Two Ostriches may never fight but still have a lot of issues – perhaps more, because they are never discussed and go unresolved. Conscious Communicators will still experience conflict, but will process it kindly and work through it with an intention to understand each other.

ACCEPTING – AND ADAPTING – YOUR FIGHT STYLE

Having a fight style doesn't make you a bad person: it makes you human. Within each of us exists a deeply embedded survival psychology that makes it natural to work to protect ourselves. Let go of any shame – our fight style is something that happens naturally, and that we can change. Better to own it and take action, than deny it and have it appear insidiously.

Bringing awareness to our style is the first step towards shifting it. For many of us, it will take a huge effort and plenty of mistakes to move into a new way of being. It's not as simple as just 'knowing'. Many of us have been relating like this for decades, and changing these habits can take time. Go gently. Have grace for yourself and your loved ones, and be sure to celebrate the small wins along the way.

One of the greatest ways to help break the cycle for others is by not engaging in the games they play. That way, they won't be successful in their attempts to draw you in. Keep bringing authenticity, vulnerability, honesty and witness awareness into your interactions. Shock them with your ability to be kind – even when it's hard. Let go of the need to defend yourself and focus on solutions.

Practice

Next time you have a fight, ask yourself which fight style you brought to the table.

Is this a common tendency for you?

What would the healthy version have looked like – what could you have done differently?

Which fight style did you see emerging in the other person?

Quiz

Look at the following list and circle the
answers that are true for you. This practice
will take radical honesty and witness
awareness. The more honest you are,
the more you will grow from this!

U = Usually
S = Sometimes
R = Rarely

You welcome difficult conversations and
are prepared to acknowledge uncomfortable
situations, rather than sweeping an issue
under the carpet.
U S R

When you begin a challenging conversation,
you have a genuine intention for resolution,
rather than just trying to win the argument.
U S R

You are able to recognise that multiple
realities can simultaneously exist, and make
an effort to listen and understand the other
person's feelings.
U S R

You don't fight dirty. When you experience conflict with another person, you are still able to behave with kindness and awareness. You stay away from hurtful one-liners, character assassinations or nasty labels.
U S R

You go gently with the insecurities and triggers of the other person.
U S R

You seek ways to solve the issue rather than focusing on winning the fight.
U S R

If the situation goes sideways, you make early attempts to make amends and repair the damage.
U S R

You are able to witness when you are emotionally flooded. You can then adjust yourself with self-regulation techniques by taking a break before things get ugly. (More on this in chapter 5.)
U S R

Owning your mistakes and apologising comes easily.
U S R

You are able to witness when you're operating from your ego, and make decisions that override the ego squeeze.
U S R

You are able to bring calm to chaos rather than chaos to chaos.
U S R

Rather than getting caught up in the little details of a fight, you are able to zoom out and look at the bigger picture.
U S R

You are able to create boundaries around how you know you deserve to be treated.
U S R

You recognise that conflict can be an opportunity for personal and or relational growth.
U S R

You know when to walk away from truly toxic scenarios.
U S R

You have learnt to pause before reacting.
U S R

You are able to witness your emotions and take the necessary steps to self-regulate.
U S R

You are able to recognise that other people's behaviour is a reflection of their inner world. You don't take their projections personally.
U S R

You are able to self-validate. You've learnt to accept that there are times when you will be misunderstood, and you're okay with that.
U S R

Take a look over your answers. Your 'Sometimes' and 'Rarelys' show honesty and self-awareness – well done on owning these! To take your witness awareness to the next level, see if you can spot this behaviour in yourself happening in real time, next time you have a challenge arise.

Your toolkit for tough times

The
Fire

5

Let's be real: sometimes, no matter how much work you've done or how far you've come, you're going to find yourself in the fire.

You may have forgotten to proceed with caution and, as a result, someone has been triggered or egos are flaring. Nervous systems are activated and the boxing gloves are on; it's getting ugly. Fights like this can do serious damage to a relationship. They chip, chip, chip away at your connection and make it increasingly hard to return unscathed to a happy place.

Not only do we want to avoid damage, but ideally, we'd like to use conflict as an opportunity for deepening our connection. When you're in the fire, you're at a crossroads moment and it could go either way. This is where we bring out the toolkit.

These tools are pure gold. In an instant, they can bring you back from conflict, landing you in a happier place where you communicate more healthily. Reaching for one of these tools may just nip the escalating conflict in the bud.

Learning to incorporate one or more of these tools into your arguments may feel awkward and vulnerable at first. It's likely that they will go against your conditioning, and they will certainly feel counterintuitive to the ego, which, as we've learned, is not such a bad thing.

You may find that some work better than others. Please note that not all of these tools are right for everyone or for every situation. With practise and time, you'll discover the tools that suit the type of arguments you have, and the person or people you're having them with. If the one you choose doesn't work, you can always reach into your toolkit and try another.

Finally, it's important to remember that sometimes the action needs to come before the feeling. We might not *feel* like using these tools to make amends, but when we do, if we can stay in that space, the feeling and intimacy will follow.

So let's give them a go.

1. Touch

When we are arguing, what happens to our body language? We look away, turn away, shut down, cross our arms. It's a natural reaction to the false egoic perception of feeling stronger by staying separate. Reaching out to touch someone during a fight is likely the opposite to what you feel like doing. However, when you physically touch a person in a gentle, comforting way, it dissolves the space between you – literally and symbolically. Instigating a calming touch can change the whole dynamic. When you can turn towards someone and soften your body language, you're opening up an option. Reaching out and touching reminds us of our togetherness, our connection. On a physiological level it can calm the nervous system and bring us out of our heads and into our bodies. But, understandably, it can take everything we've got to make that move.

So while in battle, seek awareness for an opportunity to touch. Reaching out physically, even touching their knee or shoulder, or wrapping them up in a big bear hug, can truly work magic. And if the other person doesn't want to be touched, respect their boundaries and simply try another tool out of your kit.

2. Humour

Humour is a great conflict-buster. Throwing humour in the mix can instantly defuse an argument and remind you of your togetherness. However, if you're taking this route, be careful it's not taken the wrong way. Remember, you're making a joke, but not at the other person's expense. If you can make a light joke about yourself, or a personal joke that you already share between you, you'll likely be on your way back to harmony.

3. Show you understand

Showing you understand is the easiest way to make amends. The other person may not want to be touched, and may not laugh when you joke. Showing understanding can be extremely practical and effective.

Understanding someone doesn't mean you agree with them. You don't have to tell them they're right if you don't believe they are. But by letting them know you understand where they're coming from, you are acknowledging how they feel. In a conscious argument, that's actually your responsibility: to be intentional around understanding the other person's perspective and being willing to hear opinions that are different from your own.

On the receiving end, knowing you are understood can dissolve tension immediately. Most often, we're not actually fighting to be right, but rather, to feel heard. To feel seen and heard is a basic human need. People will continue to talk until they feel heard, so be sure to be present and listen to what they have to say. Once they have explained their viewpoint, a statement such as 'I can see why you'd feel like that' can dissolve an argument instantly. Or, put even more simply, 'I understand'.

Even if you're sure you're in the right, it's helpful to acknowledge that the other person's perspective is valid. Because, for them, it is. In any disagreement, there is always more than one reality. If you were in their position, with their experience, you would feel the way they do. Put yourself in their shoes for a moment and consider how it would feel to be in their position.

'To feel seen and heard
is a basic human need.'

Tip

The next time tension builds, see how this line lands:

'I can understand why you feel like this. I think what you're saying is _____ .'

Then check to see if you've got it right. 'Is that how you feel?'

If you don't get an affirmative answer, let them explain, and then try again to understand their point of view.

Tip

You may not literally understand. Saying you understand is more about garnering an empathic intention and letting them feel that. You're saying, 'I accept that this is your reality', allowing them to have their experience in their own way.

4. Vulnerability

Showing vulnerability can help you bring each other out of your heads and into your hearts. If you can express something that shows you're dropping a barrier, and you can express it with vulnerability, you'll begin to bridge your gap. Vulnerability creates a letting down of our guard, and often creates instant intimacy. It's a beautiful way to make amends. What does showing vulnerability look like? Letting yourself be seen, even when you feel compromised. It's giving insight into how you really feel – the hurt behind the fight.

I had a client who would become triggered when his wife would walk out of the room and take space for herself when they argued. He belittled her for not having the strength to face up to their issues. When we unpacked this together in a session, he discovered he had a trigger around being abandoned. His mother had walked out on the family when he was young and left him and his sister to be raised by an aunt. When we worked together to reframe his statement to his wife and reveal, vulnerably, what he was *truly* feeling, he was able to tell her: 'I feel terrified when you walk out during an argument. It makes me scared you won't come back.' That sounds very different to belittling someone, doesn't it?

We then created a game plan for how they could manage his wife's need for space along with his fear of abandonment. And once his wife understood his fear, she was much more empathic and sensitive to his position.

It takes real courage to be vulnerable because it feels like you're exposing a weakness. It requires us to move on from a protected position to an open position. But not only will it help resolve the fight in the moment, dropping these barriers will also create more intimacy and connection in your relationship going forward.

Tip

Next time you want to turn away, lash out or close your heart down, observe this feeling within yourself and communicate it with your loved one. 'My instinct right now is to ... but I love you and I want to work through this with you.'

5. Own your shit and apologise

I once told my husband, 'I find it really sexy when you own your shit.' (Yes, it was a bit of a trick. I have discovered that whenever I tell him something is sexy, he does more of it.) But in all seriousness, there's something really attractive about someone who can say, 'I'm sorry, I acknowledge that I could have done that differently'. Or 'I messed up here'. Or 'This is how I contributed to this fight'. It takes courage to be real.

There will be times when you've clearly messed up. If this is the case, take responsibility as soon as possible. Acknowledge the impact it's had on the other person and do what you can to repair the situation.

There will also be times when you truly don't think you're at fault. Even in those moments, see if you can find anything, anywhere, for which you can take some responsibility. And let's be clear here – taking responsibility is not the same as admitting fault. You're not saying that you are wrong and the other person is right. You're simply recognising how some of your actions contributed to the situation. For example, saying 'I'm sorry I reacted so strongly. I didn't need to use that tone' can work wonders.

When you take even a small step towards taking responsibility, the other person will be more likely to do the same. Then you'll find you're moving in a positive direction.

Taking ownership is one of the most meaningful gifts you can give, but one of the hardest things to do. Your ego will try to convince you to keep fighting, but when we win at the expense of another, the relationship takes a hit. As we grow in our relationships, we recognise that resolving the situation is more important, and far more satisfying, than winning some random argument with a person we love.

6. Key statement

A simple statement is often the key to penetrating an argument and bringing us back to each other. It works as a positive trigger to remind us that love is present and we are bigger than our stuff. You may already know what your one-liner is, or maybe you're yet to discover it. Here are a few I've seen work like magic:

'Can we fix this?'

'I'd like to re-start this.'

'I can see why you would feel like that.'

'Can we hug and make up?'

'I understand what you're saying.'

'I love you more than this fight.'

'You're the most important person in my life.'

'How can I support you?'

These are a code to help you recognise that you are having an unnecessary argument or heading in that direction. You may also use it post-argument, if things are unresolved and still feeling frosty, or perhaps as a way to break through passive-aggressive treatment or stonewalling. In doing this, you're laying down your weapons and saying, 'I want to surrender this. I want us to fix this. Fixing this is more important to me than arguing.'

'Taking ownership is one
of the most meaningful
gifts you can give.'

7. Take space

Sometimes you get to a point in an argument where you're so overtaken that you have a physical, visceral reaction. Your heart rate goes up, breathing may become difficult and you feel completely overwhelmed. When you're operating in this state, you are likely to be experiencing what's called *emotional flooding*. Your adrenaline and cortisol have shot through the roof; you can't think straight, communicate clearly or easily process information.

It's unlikely that any of the above tools will break through this state. You've gone beyond the capacity for humour, intimacy, logic or creative problem-solving. You've flooded, and it's very possible that the other person has too.

Flooding may make you blow up, and you could do or say something that creates more hurt. Or perhaps you've shut down completely, making it impossible for anyone to get through to you.

Staying together in this state is going to do more damage than good. It's time to let your systems calm down and regulate. Allow some self-compassion to flood in here, too. Remind yourself it's okay to have reached this point, and seek self-care measures while you calm down. Having awareness around *how* you decide to take space will also determine the chances of recovery.

Avoid:
- Blowing up and expressing your anger in unhealthy ways. This includes leaving with a nasty one-liner, slamming the door on your way out and driving off dangerously.
- Leaving with no explanation.

Try:
- Letting the person know you are beyond reason with a code word, gesture or statement, such as:
- 'Let's take a break and try to sort this out after some space.'
- 'I'm feeling flooded.'
- 'I'm on my edge.'
- 'Let's take some space and come back when we're calmer.'

It's also helpful to have an understood timeframe for the break. 'I'm taking some space so I can calm down. I'll be back within thirty minutes.' And make sure you are.

NOTE: If you're flooded, allow at least twenty minutes to recover. This is the minimum amount of time it usually takes for your system to regulate.

WHEN YOU ARE APART

This is your time to self-regulate and calm down.
Bringing your physiology back to normal is critical.

Avoid:
- Going somewhere or doing something that will betray the other person's trust.
- Replaying the emotions and words of the fight. This will have you re-flooding yourself, and your body will think you're experiencing it again in real-time.
- Sending nasty text messages.
- Calling the person. Remember, you're taking space.
- Getting wasted. An altered mental – and physical – state delays reconciliation and signals to your loved one that they're not a priority.
- Leaving for an unknown period of time. This shows a lack of respect for the other person's time, and can create worry.

Try:
- Observing what you are experiencing physiologically. Tune into your body. Perhaps you'll notice your breath shortening, your heart beating faster, your cheeks burning. No need to judge; just observe.
- Acknowledging what you are feeling emotionally. It can be helpful to ask yourself how you're feeling and have the conversation with yourself out loud.

- Deep breathing.
- Exercise.
- Journalling.
- Something physical and methodical, like cleaning the house.
- Listening to music – play your go-to tunes that always shift your state.
- Getting yourself out in nature.

I'm not suggesting you try to bypass the emotion or suppress what you are feeling, but rather to be with it and let it flow through.

Once you've calmed down, you may begin the process of self-enquiry. Take a deep breath and ask yourself:

- 'Are the thoughts I'm having really true or is my ego attacking?' If you've noticed yourself labelling the other person – i.e. 'He's such a ...', remember to ask yourself the question 'Is that true?'
- Is there any reason not to soften? (Witness how this question brings on quite the ego squeeze!)

It's crucial to understand here that, just like you, the other person is having a physiological reaction. Their nervous system has also been triggered and is on high alert. The reason the argument is happening at that level is because your systems have signalled there is danger.

This realisation hit me hard in a fight I was having with my husband. We had an argument and he took some space, going outside to sit on our verandah.

This space allowed me to start the process of self-regulating. I reminded myself, 'You're okay, Em. You're just having a physiological reaction that has put you on high alert, because your system thinks conflict is dangerous.' All of a sudden, I realised that my husband was in exactly the same position. The reason he couldn't soften and relent, the reason he was being so intently defensive, was because his system was telling him that *conflict was dangerous*. All of a sudden, I had a deep sense of compassion for his nervous system, and for mine. I gave him some time, then went out to where he was and reached out. From that point on, we were able to speak reasonably and calmly, and sort out the issue, knowing we were both safe to express ourselves while taking care of each other.

WHEN YOU COME BACK

Avoid:
- Rushing into resolution if you're not both ready. Everybody has a different recovery time. If you walk through the door after twenty minutes wearing your heart on your sleeve and they still need time to process, you need to let them take that time.

This isn't an excuse for them to avoid resolving the issue, but simply gives them a little more space. *Try not to take this as personal rejection.* I have seen many fights re-escalate when one partner was triggered because the other person hadn't regulated within the same timeframe. If you give them a little more time, they're more likely to sort themselves and be ready to reconnect.

Try:
- If you're feeling clear, choose one of the above tools to come back with, making a game plan to help the other person regulate. You might walk through the door with a key statement ready, or arms outstretched for a hug. And this may feel ambitious enough for now.
- When you are *both* ready, revisit the conversation to work towards resolution, and then apply the 'From the Ashes' practices from Chapter 6.
- If the issue feels unresolvable even after you speak, a temporary solution may be to agree on a time to see a therapist or mediator. Taking space wasn't an excuse to sweep the issue under the carpet. Be sure to find some steps towards resolution together.

Tip

With practise, you can learn to see flooding coming. Spot the signs in yourself and the other person. My husband and I have adopted my mother's statement: 'I can feel a storm brewing.' A one-liner like this can bring both people's awareness to the reactive or defensive stance you're taking with each other.

HAVE A FLOODING GAME PLAN

Remember our couple from earlier? She would need space during a fight, but this would trigger her partner's fear of abandonment. Once we put a game plan in place, both of them were able to have the experience they required, which in turn helped them better resolve their conflicts.

In connections where flooding sometimes occurs, it is extremely helpful to agree on a Flooding Game Plan. Discuss what you both need to feel safe based on the above information. Perhaps you pre-agree on:

- which person will stay and which person will leave
- the amount of time you both feel comfortable being separated for
- what you both feel okay with happening while separated
- a process for when one of you is not regulated when the other is ready to talk.

If you have a predefined Flooding Game Plan, taking space will not be perceived as a personal attack on the other person. Instead, it will be mutually recognised as a healthy and necessary step towards reconciliation.

Tip

It's helpful to take space *before* flooding occurs and to re-engage when you're feeling calmer. I can't emphasise this enough. Go for a short walk around the block to help you regulate your emotions the moment you notice them surfacing. Alternatively, you can put this plan in place *before* you begin a challenging conversation. Agree to allow each person to speak their thoughts, then take twenty to sixty minutes to separate, do your own thing, then come back together once you've had time to process both perspectives.

Tip

If only one of you has flooded, there is the potential for the non-flooded person to help soothe the other. If this is the case, you may not need to take the space. If you are flooded and your partner isn't, try to communicate this:

'I'm feeling flooded. I need help right now.'

'I'm really triggered. Can you be my rock?'

If you're the non-flooded person and you know the other person well, you may already know what they need. If you're unsure of what to do, you can simply ask them: 'How can I best help you right now?'

Self-regulation – on-the-spot

Conflict is challenging, and as we evolve our relationships, we empower ourselves to feel emotions and soothe ourselves through these difficult experiences. Slowly we see that conflict isn't always dangerous. It becomes less painful when we learn to take it less personally. By re-wiring our reaction patterns, we learn to relate more maturely.

When you hone the superpower of on-the-spot self-regulation, you're able to find your centre even while at the centre of a challenging situation.

By stepping back and recognising your emotions as they arise, you remain clear-headed, are proactive rather than reactive, and prevent yourself from shutting down or blowing up. See what I mean by superpower?

With practise, we can learn to become aware of when we're being dysregulated, then turn the tables so we regulate during triggering interactions. And the more you stabilise yourself, the more stable your relationships become.

Self-regulation helps us stay connected to our loved ones during arguments or difficult conversations, and is a game-changing tool when we're dealing with those who haven't yet learnt how to consciously communicate.

And the best bit? All you need is you. Let's make a start now.

Practice

Try the following self-regulation techniques:

- Before you respond, pause. This allows space to be proactive, not reactive.
- As you listen, fill your belly with deep breaths. Focus on it expanding as you inhale, and relaxing as you exhale.
- Focus on your physical body and become deeply present. Notice your feet on the earth, wiggle your toes, and move your awareness to your fingertips.
- Anchor yourself in your body. Place a hand on your heart, on your tummy, or hold one palm in the other.
- Be curious about your emotions. Internally name them. 'I feel disappointed.'
- Be curious about any sensations, too. 'My heart is racing.'
- Soothe with an internal mantra. It might be a direct pep talk, like: 'It makes sense that I am feeling overwhelmed right now.' Or a message from your higher self, like: 'It's okay, beautiful, I'm here for you.'

NOTE: Sometimes it's too late for on-the-spot self-soothing. For those moments, remember to seek some time out.

FLOODING CHEAT SHEET

This is HARD. Right now, you may be fuming, shaking or crying. Perhaps your heart is beating rapidly or your legs feel wobbly. And it SUCKS.

Whatever you are feeling at this moment, don't try to change it. Be right there in it.

Just watch. Observe your physiology and say out loud – what can you feel in your body? Don't try to fight it; just let it be there.

Now, put your hand on your belly. Take a slow deep breath in through your nose and fill your belly up so it expands. Exhale slowly through your mouth and let your belly drop back.

You're doing great.

Let's go again, and this time, count.

Inhale for four, exhale for six.

Make a sound as you exhale.

Repeat three more times, or as many as it feels right.

Feel the ground beneath your feet (or bottom).

Feel the earth beneath you.

Look around and tell me out loud five things that you can see.

Tell me what you can hear.

Tell me what you physically feel.

Feeling a little more grounded?

Spend the next twenty minutes doing something for you. Clean your house, go for a brisk walk, put on a tune you love and let your body move. As you're doing this, notice how your body feels. Become aware of your thoughts – notice if the mind is creating a story and becoming attached to it, or if the ego is labelling something or someone.

Then come back and read on.

If you've noticed yourself labelling the other person – i.e. 'He's such a ...', remember to ask the question 'Is that true?'

Is there any reason not to soften?

If you're not quite ready for these questions, come back to the breath. Big inhale, and a loud sound or sigh on the exhale. Let it out.

When you are feeling ready to come back to a conversation with the person you felt triggered by, try using the Aftermath Cheat Sheet in Chapter 6 to keep the conversation conscious and on track.

Tip

Take a photo of these pages and keep them on your phone, or carefully tear these pages out of the book and pop them in your wallet or phone case. Keep them somewhere handy where you'll have easy access to them.

Five fire stoppers

Ignite only one issue at a time

Be careful not to confuse the current issue with new problems or past grievances, or by pointing out personal flaws. If multiple arguments arise, agree to talk about them separately once you have resolved the current topic.

Lower your walls

Arguments are often caused or perpetuated by someone's (or both people's) defensiveness. When we can remain curious and open to the perspectives of others, we become safe and approachable. If you are highly defensive, people will not want to approach you. It becomes 'too hard' to talk to you, but the issues don't disappear. They often turn into something far more dangerous and damaging to our connections: resentment. So be sure to soften your walls, breathe deep and adopt an open mind.

During conflict, do you have a tendency to defend yourself intently? Do you remain open to the opinions and perspectives of ohers? Or do you shut them down immediately and defend your position to death?

Re-commit to kindness

We've talked about fighting dirty, and how it is possible to feel challenged, angry, hurt, frustrated and even flooded without getting nasty. If you notice your tone has become aggressive, or you're pointing out personal flaws, using other people's opinions for leverage, naming names, aiming for soft spots or getting mean, you're fighting dirty.

In conscious relationships, we choose to bring calm to the chaos rather than throwing down verbal hand grenades. The person you're talking to is a human with a soul inside their body. They deserve love, kindness, respect and your manners, just as you deserve the same in return.

Do you have a tendency to fight dirty during conflict? What are the ways you do this?

Have you felt the urge to fight dirty during conflict, but managed to refrain from doing so? How did that feel?

Tip

Remember that you are only responsible for your own emotions and behaviour. Other people's behaviour is a reflection of *their* internal world. If someone is behaving in a way that is spiteful or nasty, this isn't personal; it simply gives you some insight into the inner workings of their mind.

Solve both sides

Rather than focusing on the problem, put your energy into the solution. If you keep hitting brick walls, pause and zoom out for a moment to look at what the other person wants. Name the problem in simple terms, then take turns to each come up with one or two suggestions that you think could solve the problem. This shift in conversation can alter our focus from feeling separate to feeling like team players navigating each other's needs. From this mindset you are more likely to uncover the creative solution that was there all along.

Advance with empathy

As wild as it may sound, it is possible to not only fight kindly, but to also have empathy for the person who is challenging you. You can support the other person during an intense conversation, and help them to regulate by listening, acknowledging their reality and reaching into your toolkit. They'll have less to fight for when they know you care about them and are prepared to feel their pain and understand their side.

'In conscious relationships, we choose to bring calm to the chaos rather than throwing down verbal hand grenades.'

Practice

Breath is one of the fastest ways to regulate our nervous system and shift our mindset. When we change our breath, we change our minds. Any time you feel agitated, anxious or tense, use the following practice to come back to your calm.

1. Sit in a comfortable position and place your hands on your belly.
2. Take a long deep breath in through your nose. As you do, inhale all the way down to your belly and fill it with your breath. If you're doing this correctly, you'll notice that your belly gently expands.
3. Hold the breath for three seconds.
4. Exhale slowly through the mouth.
5. Repeat anywhere between 3–10 times.

By focusing on the breath for this short period of time, you've brought yourself into the present moment and given your mind and your system a gentle reset. When the practice of pausing, breathing and grounding becomes your default, it's a game changer.

What happens next

From
the Ashes

6

You'll find real potential for growth in the aftermath of a fight. As tempting as it may be to just move on, there's now space for you to undo any damage done and to learn valuable lessons for next time. It can be common for one or both of you to feel more upset about the way you fought, rather than what you fought about, so decompressing can help to identify these details.

How you handle these damaged dregs can make all the difference for both your present interactions and your future conflicts. Try seeing this as a necessary stage of conflict resolution, and approach it with care and curiosity.

Acknowledge that multiple realities exist

I can't reiterate this one enough: multiple realities exist. So many conflicts are the result of two people simply having two different experiences of the same event.

I have a huge painting that hangs on the wall of my house, and I love it dearly. It is an abstract piece of work that I commissioned, and it contains symbology that represents the core values and culture of our little family. When this piece arrived, I hung it on the wall and it made my heart sing. A girlfriend came around to visit, and when she saw the painting she thought my three-year-old son had painted it. My husband found this hilarious, and my girlfriend couldn't believe how much money I had spent on it. Two days later, another girlfriend came to my house, saw the painting and was blown away. She recognised the artist and went into great detail describing the brilliance of the work. Two different reactions, both completely valid. Neither of my girlfriends was wrong; they simply had different realities of the same experience.

When you come back together after a fight, I suggest one or both of you say out loud:

'Let's first acknowledge that multiple realities exist.'
Then:

'What did your reality of the situation look like?'

As the other person describes their reality, listen. *Really* listen, and imagine yourself seeing the experience from their perspective. This isn't about right or wrong; you're simply being given a front row seat to their experience. Could you imagine, if you were in their shoes, with their personality, how they might have had that experience? (Note: at this stage, your ego may desperately want to hold onto the drama and make the other person wrong – watch for the squeeze here.)

Then it's your turn. 'What my reality looked like was ...'

It's important that both people's feelings are heard. How they are feeling is how they are feeling. When we grow in emotional maturity, we learn to stop invalidating other people's experiences.

Tip

If possible, implement this practice when you're in the fire. The sooner you use this step, the faster you'll move towards reconciliation.

What I did to contribute

I have found, both personally and when working with clients, that for one person to point out all the things the other person *should* have done, in the hope they will change, is often fruitless. It is likely to trigger the other person's ego and its need to defend itself. Rather than pointing out what someone did wrong, I suggest each of you takes responsibility, offering your personal reflections on your own behaviour. Take turns saying 'On reflection, the ways I contributed to this were ...' It's a far more empowering move, and when we own our actions, we're more likely to create change.

So, own your shit. It's the sexy thing to do.

Map your war zone

Mapping out your war zone is an essential part of this process. It's where you'll experience the light-bulb moments that show you what to look out for next time.

Jason doesn't operate well under pressure, so instead of supporting Claire, who needed help to meet an important work deadline, he started to crack under the building tension. This then set off Claire's trigger, which is feeling unsupported during tough times. Things went pear-shaped when Jason got snappy. Claire couldn't believe he was speaking to her in that tone at a time when she felt he should be supporting her. They had a huge blow-up and Jason stormed out, leaving Claire to fume.

By mapping their war zone, Claire and Jason learned to flag the conditions in which they are most likely to have a fight.

Here are some conditions that may contribute to a potential war zone:

- One or both parties are under stress.
- One or both parties are tired or hungry.
- One or both parties hasn't practiced self-love or self-care for some time.
- When there hasn't been conflict for some time. (This one is particularly potent if one or both parties is addicted to drama.)
- Family get-togethers.
- Holidays and important dates.
- Lack of sexual connection in an intimate relationship.
- Differences in opinion – about how to raise children, lifestyle choices, extended family relationships, money or housework, to name a few!

What are the conditions in which you tend to argue with your loved ones?

What are your triggers? What are your loved one's triggers?

MOVING FORWARD

To move forward, Claire and Jason created a plan.

'This is the type of situation in which we have fought in the past. Let's have awareness and go very gently with each other. Let's take care not to take things personally and to be considerate, tender and kind.'

Aware that Jason is overwhelmed by high-pressure situations, Claire agreed to create more space around deadlines. They also acknowledged that life will throw down unavoidable challenges, so Jason made a commitment to practice self-regulation, take care of himself and be careful not to project his stress onto Claire. Claire created a boundary around Jason's tone of voice. They agreed that when they are in their war-zone conditions, they will flag it.

They put themselves on the same team. They are on the lookout for each other's triggers, and they are supporting each other to manage a situation that has historically caused them problems.

In mapping your war zone, two important things are happening. By taking a moment to state how you would do things differently, you increase the chance that next time you *will* do things differently. This is part of the process of changing old habits, patterns and learned behaviours. The other thing that's happening is you've transmuted the situation, turning a conflict into a deeper relationship connection.

WRAP IT UP WITH LOVE

End on a loving note. Wrap it up by reminding yourselves of why you're in a relationship with each other, and apply a soothing balm to each other's nervous systems.

Take turns with:

'Three things I love about you are ...'

NOTE: If the person you are doing this process with is someone you don't feel intimate with, you can replace the word 'love' with 'appreciate' or 'admire'.

Fighting isn't fun for anyone, but by being more conscious within our challenges, we can begin to shift our endless cycles of conflict and unresolved disputes. That's a desirable disruption.

Tip

Take a mental picture of your loved one in a moment where you're feeling particularly loving, grateful or appreciative of them. Try to remember this image when you've spiralled into a negative story about them. It can help to balance your view. Take note, however, that in the heat of the moment, your ego won't want to conjure up this picture. So, write it down on the back of the flooding cheat sheet towards the end of Chapter 5.

Practice

Our brains naturally have a negativity bias. This is due to ancestral survival psychology in which paying attention to pessimistic possibilities and negative past experiences increased the likelihood of survival. If you are experiencing a challenging phase in your relationship or recovering from a hurtful interaction, you'll likely be even more on the lookout for potential pain, or perhaps be oversensitive to your loved one's words and actions. Create a practice with your loved one to, at the end or start of the day, let them know one thing you love about them. Do this for at least one week. This simple exercise will help direct the brain towards acknowledging what is good and wonderful, and will help the healing process. Gratitude acts as a magnet, so be sure to acknowledge the experiences or qualities you want more of in your relationships. You will find that over time, these experiences are more likely to amplify when you express appreciation and gratitude for what is working.

Aftermath cheat sheet

Let's be honest. A good portion of the information in this chapter may fly right out the window when you're feeling emotional or navigating your way back from conflict. Use the following as a guide when you're cleaning up after a fight, and let me take you through the process as though I'm in the room. Be sure to dog-ear this page so you can easily find it in the moment, and stick with the process, because it works!

Acknowledge that multiple realities exist

'Let's first acknowledge that multiple realities exist.'

Then:

Person 1: 'What did your reality of the situation look like?'

Person 2: 'What did your reality of the situation look like?'

Remember: It's important we hold space for other people's viewpoints, even if they're different to ours.

What I did to contribute

Person 1: 'On reflection, the ways I contributed to this were...........'

Person 2: 'On reflection, the ways I contributed to this were...........'

Map your war zone

- What were the conditions this fight happened in?
- What were the triggers?

Moving forward

- How would we do it differently next time?
- Do we need to create a boundary around this?
- What do we commit to?
- What have we learned from this experience?

Loving practice

Person 1: 'Three things I love/appreciate about you are ...'

Person 2: 'Three things I love/appreciate about you are ...'

Conflict manifesto

We have learnt a lot and journeyed far. It's now time to reflect on some of the lessons we've gathered.

I'm going to ask you to come up with your own conflict manifesto by identifying the important lessons, truth bombs or concepts you want to take with you.

Start by scanning through the statements below and circle the ones that stand out or strike a chord. Once you've finished your circling, re-write the statements consecutively into a paragraph at the back of the book or in a journal. This then becomes your manifesto, a declaration of your intentions and ideas around how you'd like to handle and integrate conflicts and challenges in your relationship/s.

Conflict manifesto statements

- Conflict is a gateway to personal growth.
- We can disagree and still stay connected.
- I will lean into the lesson that this can bring.
- I endeavour to see the perspective of the other.
- I understand that multiple realities can exist.
- I understand their feelings are valid.

- I will be curious rather than defensive.
- I don't need to prove myself.
- It's okay to be misunderstood.
- I will question the stories my mind creates.
- I will question if I am projecting my own personal pain onto another.
- I will bring awareness to my tendencies, behaviours and triggers.
- I endeavour to listen with presence and communicate with kindness.
- I will seek creative solutions that will serve both parties.
- We can have different opinions, yet still have a calm and mature experience.
- I will ask questions before making assumptions.
- Others deserve to be treated with respect.
- I don't need to take other people's feelings and actions personally.
- I can let go of old resentments and grievances, and start again.
- I can self-soothe and stay calm.
- I am responsible for my responses.
- We can grow through what we go through.
- I am willing to listen without trying to control.
- I will let them say their piece without interrupting or overriding.
- I will have compassion for their triggers, and be sensitive to their vulnerabilities.
- I can be empathic, even when I'm hurting.

- I will observe how my ego wants to remain separate and make them wrong.
- I know I make mistakes, and I endeavour to own them.
- I am prepared to apologise.
- Conflict is not a disaster, and does not signal the end of the relationship.
- I am willing to be vulnerable.
- I am willing to reach out to make amends, despite the ego squeeze that may bring.
- I will endeavour to keep my heart open, even when it wants to shut down.
- Staying conscious during conflict is a spiritual practice.
- Breathe.

The word 'manifesto' is related to the word 'manifest'. Which is essentially the point of your manifesto – to manifest a new way of experiencing the challenges and tough times in relationships. By writing, reading and re-reading your conflict manifesto, you are teaching yourself to redefine your challenges and become a conscious communicator (remember the fight styles in Chapter 4?). It's a map that helps re-wire the way you respond to challenging experiences with others. Make yours as simple or as detailed as you want.

'Fighting isn't fun for anyone, but by being more conscious within our challenges, we can begin to shift our endless cycles of conflict and unresolved disputes.'

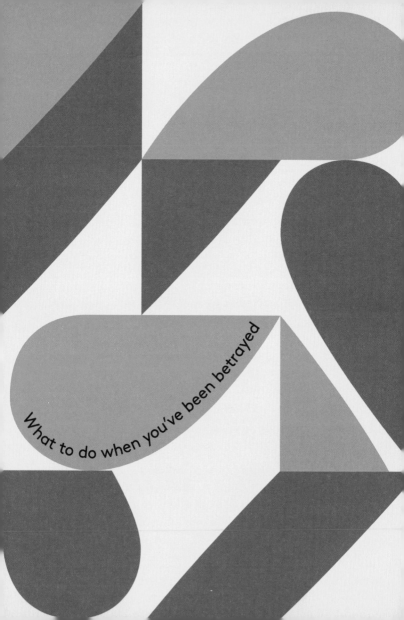
What to do when you've been betrayed

Forgiveness

7

You won't find forgiveness in a one-size-fits-all package. There's no standard formula that is right for everyone. There are different levels to what we choose to forgive, and different depths to how we've been affected.

So rather than considering forgiveness as an all-or-nothing experience, let's see it as a scale. At one end is the first step towards forgiveness. This starts with choosing to reclaim your energy from the situation. It's an initial gesture that begins with accepting that what has happened cannot be changed. Although your feelings of hurt or anger are valid, you're ready to feel something different.

At the other end of the scale is complete forgiveness, the type where we forgive and forget. The experience is in the past and no longer infiltrates the present. For many of us, complete forgiveness is far beyond the scope of what we're ready for, and may not be an appropriate response. Waiting to get to this point can keep us stuck.

Consider stepping onto the scale as an act of self-love. We've been hurt by someone, something or a situation, and it wasn't okay. But not only were we hurt then, we continue to be hurt now. It has attached to us, occupying our mental real estate and taking our precious energy. The first step comes when we say enough is enough. When we recognise we need to move on, to let go, *for our own sake*. We realise that by holding onto resentment, we're doing ourselves damage. This realisation allows us to release the grip that person or situation has on us. We consciously cut the energetic cords that have been binding us to the past, and reclaim our energy.

On the other end is the total expression of forgiveness. At this level, we forgive not only to free ourselves, but also the other person. This is not only an act of self-love but also one of unconditional love. When we forgive in this way, we forgive and forget. We wipe the slate clean, let go of the past completely and begin with a fresh start. This is an act of grace – giving without expectation of reciprocation – and is often an expression of the heart. An example of this is a parent forgiving their child when they say something spiteful. Full forgiveness often happens in relationships that are ongoing, or where we know the other person deeply. In that situation, it's easier to see them as a whole person, and the hurtful action as something they've done, as opposed to who they are entirely.

In some cases, once we step onto the Forgiveness Scale, we start to inch along it. We find that time or circumstances shift how we feel. Reclaiming our energy can lead towards further forgiveness down the track, when wounds heal or we find more clarity.

Take a client of mine, Carly. After she had her first baby, she fell out with her sister. Her sister was overjoyed to be an aunt, but this excitement caused her to be pushy and opinionated. She made comments and demands that were painful and unfair. It created drama at a time where Carly was already under pressure as a new mum. Carly felt that this precious time, when she wanted to bond with her baby, was consumed with family conflict. She started having dark feelings towards her sister.

Carly realised her energy was being consumed and drained by her hurt and anger, and she decided it was time to feel something different. We worked together on ways to reclaim her feelings and thoughts. She made decisions about the boundaries she needed to put in place to feel protected in her vulnerable state. Two years on, Carly has a respectful and lovely relationship with her sister. They put the past behind them, and the boundaries Carly put in place gave them both clarity on the direction and shape of their relationship. By reclaiming her energy first, Carly felt better about spending time with her sister again, gaining perspective and even empathy for her.

There will be times where we make progress along the scale. We may also never get beyond that first step, and that's okay too.

Forgiveness isn't easy

Forgiveness can sometimes feel awkward and unnatural, so it's important to go easy on ourselves.

As we've learned, the ego thrives on separateness. A part of you may not want to forgive. If you were wronged by someone who you didn't particularly like, on some level you may even be celebrating an excuse to throw emotional ammo their way. Remember to recognise the difference between the very real experience, and the point where the ego is trying to kick in. Acknowledge the reality of what you've experienced without amplifying it with drama and stories.

Motivation to mend

Forgiveness benefits your physical, emotional and mental wellbeing. When a lack of forgiveness is spiking, so too are your stress hormones. When someone hurts you, your sympathetic nervous system launches into action, and tries to protect you by preparing to fight or flee. Your heart is racing, your blood pressure spikes and your immune system is compromised.

By inviting forgiveness in, we can be kind to our bodies. We can begin to heal. A Harvard Medical School study showed that forgiveness can lower levels of depression, anxiety and hostility, reduce substance abuse, boost self-esteem and give greater life satisfaction.

We've already learned how stepping onto the Forgiveness Scale helps us reclaim our energy and headspace. We can find further motivation to forgive by recognising that resentment can negatively infiltrate other areas of our life. It creates a distorted lens through which we may see people's actions based on our past hurts and experiences. This warped view can make us behave in a way that sabotages our connections. Forgiveness brings us back into the present, and into the arms of our loved ones.

Overcoming the obstacles

So we've stepped onto our position on the Forgiveness Scale and we want to get started. A word of warning: there may be obstacles on your course.

WAITING FOR AN APOLOGY

It's natural to expect an apology when someone does something wrong. We need some sort of remittance or acknowledgement of their transgression to move on.

But as long as you are relying on the other person to apologise, you are tied to them. The power is in their hands because they have the choice to say sorry – or not. Here's the unfortunate truth: most people who do wrong don't want to acknowledge their wrongdoing. Not to themselves, and certainly not to another. So while it's a helpful bonus if they *do* apologise, don't wait for them to validate your reality. Take your life and energy into your own hands by choosing freedom and cutting the ties that bind you to their behaviour.

Maybe the apology will come, maybe it won't. But their journey and conscience is their business. Don't keep your life on hold due to someone else's inability to apologise. When you are ready to heal, you don't need anyone else's permission to start.

HOPING FOR REVENGE

It's common to want the person who hurt you to experience some kind of retribution. Unfortunately, this won't lead to freedom, peace or inner strength. Again, you are relying on something outside of yourself to give you a sense of closure. Let it go.

When we look at true freedom as stepping into our power, we understand that those who can't apologise aren't truly free. They are holding themselves back from connecting, and limiting themselves by hurting others. Taking ownership for the pain we've caused and making amends is a way to truly grow in our relationships – with others and ourselves.

THINKING YOU HAVE TO LIKE THEM AFTERWARDS

You don't. Forgiveness doesn't mean friendship. It doesn't offer respect and it doesn't mean you have to want to be around the other person. You may never see that person again, and if you do, you aren't obligated to extend yourself towards them. So don't put pressure on yourself. You're simply letting go, not becoming besties. The level of reconciliation and type of relationship you are ready for is in your hands. You have the power.

Stepping onto the scale

Ask yourself: 'Am I ready to forgive?' This is an essential first step. You don't need to *try* to forgive someone. Rushing your way to completion can have you emotionally bypassing important steps in the forgiveness process and squelching your feelings into a state of denial. The goal here is to truly let go. This is not the place to filter your experience to save their feelings. That's their work to do.

It may feel vulnerable to sit with your pain, and uncomfortable to be with your intense emotions. It's important not to deny or ignore your real feelings. It is completely valid to feel angry and hurt when someone has wronged you. You have every right to seek justice for their actions. You are entitled to create boundaries around your energy and time, or choose to no longer have this person in your life. Be sure to let your anger and pain have the airtime it deserves.

Beware of burying your hurt or anger. This is a short-term fix, and with time, the buried pain will build to a mountain. While it may feel like you're letting go, you're actually pushing the pain deeper into your body – and your heart. You're tightening the hurt on your soul.

This is where we can have our own back. There are steps we can take to support us in our process, and reach a place where we are more likely to step onto the Forgiveness Scale.

1. ACCEPTANCE

What has happened has happened. It can't be changed. This recognition immediately brings us to the beginning of our process. What happened may have been earth-shattering, mind-blowingly painful. You're likely thinking, 'It should never have happened', but we need to recognise that it *has*. There may be a rollercoaster of emotions to move through before you get to that place – like anger, depression, frustration and pain. But at some point, in order to heal, you need to accept. You do NOT need to accept it was okay; you are simply entering the acceptance phase and looking ahead to what's next.

2. CLARITY

Get clear on the specifics of the issue, as well as its impact on your life. For example, if you experienced a betrayal, acknowledge genuinely how it has affected you. What ripple effect did the act of betrayal have on your inner and outer world? Perhaps it affected your ability to trust. It may have broken up your family. It might have severed friendships. Although this step can be painful, it's important to acknowledge exactly what is in need of healing. There's no point pretending a very real wound is simply a scratch.

3. MOVEMENT

Once, the term 'fight or flight' literally meant what it indicates – when feeling confronted we would physically fight, or we would flee. In doing so, we would process the surge of cortisol in our body by releasing it through movement. These days, a lot of our fight or flight happens verbally or cognitively, and therefore the stress stays stored in our physical structure.

So let's shake it off. Movement helps to release the emotions you have around an event. This will look different for every person, but as long as your endorphins are flowing, you're doing it right. Perhaps you get your kicks from running, boxing, dancing or yoga. Or maybe you're keen to try something new, like Trauma Release Exercises or Somatic Dance Therapy. Breathwork can also be incredibly helpful to regulate your nervous system.

4. COMMUNICATION

Share your experience with trusted loved ones who can hold you and your vulnerabilities through it, or a professional who will create space for your process. Talking about what you have been through and expressing the associated emotions can help you to feel heard and understood.

Be mindful there can come a point where you may be keeping your experience alive by compulsively retelling your story, both to yourself and others. This can keep you in the role of victim and prevent you from moving on. Be sure to use discretion when choosing who to share your experience with. Are the people you're talking to genuinely helping you process your experience? Or are they exacerbating the situation by stirring up your feelings and aggravating things further? Keep in mind there may come a time where you're ready to move on, but your support network isn't.

5. HONESTY

Ask yourself if you genuinely want to move on. Take a quiet moment of self-reflection and ask yourself:

- Am I ready to accept and move past the situation?
- Do I feel more powerful by holding on to unforgiveness?
- Am I exaggerating the circumstances?

There's no need to judge yourself or your answers. The intention here is to simply witness what is truly going on for you. Don't try to change your feelings; the very act of acknowledging them is the work itself. Remember there is a process here, and some of these feelings are a necessary part of it.

6. PERSPECTIVE

It's important to recognise that people are unable to behave beyond their current level of consciousness. A large portion of our pain comes from personalising someone's unconscious behaviour. This isn't about you. It's about them. If you expand your thinking to consider where they have come from, what they have inherited from their parents and where their triggers lie, you will see that the way they are behaving is a reflection of their inner world. People are usually acting from unhealed emotional wounds rather than malicious intent. This doesn't mean you don't have boundaries and standards around the way you are treated. It just means you take it less personally.
It can help to see the person who has hurt you from two perspectives. There's the side where they hurt you, acted cruelly, did wrong by you and acted out of order. Then there's the other side, where they have inherited trauma, have fears, have unconscious behavioural patterns and haven't been exposed to opportunities to grow. Or perhaps they are currently experiencing a lot of pressure, pain or fear. Don't diminish your pain or let them off the hook. Instead, bring perspective to the situation.

7. PLAN

What are the practical next steps? How are you going to move forward from here? There will be times when you genuinely need to protect yourself or seek justice for what has happened. Putting boundaries in place, drawing the line on behaviours you'll no longer tolerate or seeking retribution is valid, and can be an important part of the process. It's something you can do without reproach and while forgiving.

You might make an appointment with a marriage counsellor, or maybe you need to take legal action. Being proactive will help you move towards a solution.

Further, there is a lesson in every situation. A positive outcome that often comes from painful situations is the steps we take to look after ourselves in the aftermath.

8. EMPATHY

When someone has hurt us, we have a tendency to demonise them. Instead, try to remind yourself they are a human and they make mistakes – just like you. Be honest with yourself about the size of the event. Take into consideration the ratio of good to bad when it comes to their personhood.

Remind yourself of the little things that make them normal. I remember being mad at a relative who hurt me once, and then looking down and seeing his shoes at the door and thinking there was something so vulnerable and normal about them. It reminded me he was human too. It can sometimes be helpful to be in the same place as the person who has hurt you. Being reminded of their humanness can cultivate compassion and empathy. This can be useful when you have turned the person into a monstrous ogre in your mind.

NOTE: This is not always safe or appropriate, so consider whether this is right for you and your circumstances.

NOTE: I'm not suggesting that understanding the 'why' behind someone's actions or empathising with their position excuses their behaviour. No way. You can be compassionate without being a doormat. You can understand their behaviour without allowing it to continue.

9. SELF-ACCEPTANCE

Just because you feel like you've forgiven your offender one day doesn't mean you'll feel the same way the next. Forgiveness doesn't mean you will never again feel emotions about the event. Allow space for your feelings and thoughts. Let them come and go without judgement. They may need to swirl around and rear back up before they can clear.

10. STRENGTHENING

Steer your attention away from the person or event and instead bring yourself back to the present moment. Every time you ruminate on your past – the events that have happened, what that person did to you, how much they've hurt you, how angry you are – you're draining your available energy and sending it their way. You're also reinforcing the neural pathways that keep taking you back there.

Strengthen the mind by practising witness awareness, mindfulness and meditation, and using mantras or affirmations. As you continue to bring your mind and energy back to focus on the present, the old pathways of pain will weaken and eventually drop away. As they do so, you will begin to taste the freedom that comes from letting go of your past. Eventually, new circuitry can be established and you will be free from the grip the event or person has on you.

Use this step if you notice you are incessantly overthinking or you feel mentally stuck, but not as a method of denial or emotional bypassing. Letting your feelings ebb and flow as they naturally process is important, as is expressing your dark and painful emotions about the situation.

Practice

When emotions about the event or person surface again, use the witness awareness practice from Chapter 1 to observe what you're feeling without judgement.

Ask yourself:

'What am I feeling right now?' (Example: 'I am feeling angry and hurt.')

'How does my body feel?' (Example: 'My heart is beating fast and I'm finding it hard to breathe.')

You may need to return to this exercise a number of times as your feelings surface and resurface, and new emotions present themselves.

Practice

Bring yourself back to the present with the simple breath mindfulness technique offered on page 157.

Burning ceremony

If you feel that you're ready to let go and reclaim your energy back, you can practice the following ritual.

You will need:
- a small piece of paper, pen, candle, matches, a fireproof dish or bowl.
- additional options: a sage smudge stick, fresh flowers/leaves.

Step 1: Prepare the space

Place the candle, dish and flowers all in the one place. Make yourself comfortable on a cushion or chair, have your pen, paper and matches by your side.

Step 2: Get centred

It's important that you feel grounded, centred and calm before you start the ritual. Light your candle, then take three deep breaths into your belly to help bring you into a present state.

Step 3: Get clear

Write on your piece of paper what it is you're letting go of. This may be a person or a situation.

Step 4: Burn

Hold the paper over the flame, then, once you're sure it's burning, drop the paper into the fireproof receptacle. Remember fire safety here! Be sure to watch the entire paper burn.

Step 5: Finish

Finish your ritual with a visualisation. Close your eyes and imagine your energy returning to you. Keep your eyes closed and place both of your hands on your heart. Seal the practice by taking one final deep breath into your heart, and allow yourself to smile. When you open your eyes, notice the shift in your state.

We won't always understand why things happen, but while we can't change the past and we can't change other people, we can change the way we move forward. We can forgive.

Forgiveness is a powerful tool to help us break the cycles we've been repeating and to place boundaries on what we tolerate. Armed with forgiveness, we can tend to our wounds and heal on our own terms. Let's take back the reins on our own existence and lovingly steer ourselves in the direction that best serves us. For us.

7: FORGIVENESS

Seeking forgiveness?

- Own your mistakes and apologise.
- Don't try to minimise their pain.
- Consider the bigger picture. Acknowledge the effects of your actions.
- Take practical steps towards retribution. Channel your guilt into positive action.
- Be patient. There will often be waves of processing for the other person. You may think you've been forgiven, only for the issue to arise again. This is often a vital aspect of the healing journey and it's important to allow it.
- Learn from your mistakes. If you are given another opportunity to prove yourself, step up to the plate.
- Be sensitive to the circumstances. Tread carefully in situations that could re-trigger pain and open old wounds.
- If appropriate, suggest that you attend professional therapy together.
- Know your personal boundaries around the circumstance. You don't deserve to be endlessly punished. You'll need to have a lot of grace, but it's not an excuse for abuse or manipulation. Be sure the steps you take towards reconciliation feel like the right thing to do.

'Holding onto anger is like grasping a hot coal with the intent of throwing it at someone else; you are the one who gets burned.'

Growing and pruning

Making
Change

8

Every relationship has its own distinctive culture. A tone, an energy, a way of being that, without much thought or focus, seems to be 'just how things are'. Perhaps you struggle to show your feelings, or maybe your intimate partnership feels like it's fallen into a complacent rut. Maybe you're in a bitchy workplace, or a friendship that feels co-dependent. Just because it's like that right now doesn't mean it always has to be. It only takes one person – in the family, or the couple, the workplace or the friendship – to inspire a shift in the patterns and encourage a new way of being.

However, it's also important to understand and recognise that you can't change another person. You can't talk them into changing, you can't love them into changing, you can't manipulate them to change, and you can't tell them they have to. *They will only change if they want to.* They have to feel a stirring, a genuine impetus. Otherwise their change is a pretence, and it will only last so long. And when the facade drops, they'll likely resent you for forcing their hand, and you'll resent them for being the same as they always were.

So, what do we do when someone won't change? YOU DO YOU.

As Aldous Huxley said, 'There is only one corner of the universe you can be certain of improving, and that's your own self.'

Rather than channelling energy into pain, frustration and anger towards the one we want to change, let's call that energy back to ourselves. Let's turn inwards and quietly get to work. That 'work' is simply about meeting yourself, again and again, and discovering who you really are. It's understanding that to evolve is our nature. Our relationships (and our reactivity) are our teachers. It's loving and nourishing the heck out of yourself, having grace and compassion for yourself, gently taking yourself by your own hand and staying true to your own path. It's learning what your boundaries are and laying them down.

When we reconnect to ourselves, we stop betraying ourselves. We no longer believe another will 'complete' us. We no longer stay in relationships for appearance, appeasement, out of fear or habit.

8: MAKING CHANGE

Rather than needing or seeking someone or something outside of yourself to be a certain way, you're filling your cup, feeling secure, self-assured and stable. You'll be rewarded – regardless of what happens in the relationship itself – by stepping closer to your true self and honouring your own journey.

If others don't want to come along for the ride, that may be the magical indicator – and motivator – it's time for us to do our personal work, more than ever.

Doing the inner work

As you do the work on yourself, your relationship with yourself and others will inevitably transform. You may experience the following:

You step back and realise how you've been contributing to conflict

Have you ever looked back at a past relationship with an ex or a friend and recognised how you could have done things differently? Where perhaps you were part of the problem, too? At the time, you were pointing fingers, or lacking grace. But with perspective, you can recognise that it wasn't entirely their fault.

'Knowing others is intelligence; knowing yourself is true wisdom. Mastering others is strength; mastering yourself is true power.'

Sometimes we contribute to the very dynamic that is causing our pain. We hurt others. We push away love. We avoid intimacy. We model unhealthy behaviour. We repeat destructive patterns. We have our triggers, trauma, stories, shadow traits and projections. We get stuck in our heads and we shut down our hearts.

When we do our own work, we may recognise these things about ourselves *in real-time*, instead of five years down the track when reflecting on our past connections. The light bulb goes off in the moment. And then we get to apply the learning from the lesson.

You may inspire change in others through the changes in yourself

It's not the motivation for making these changes, but it's a possible outcome. Doing the work, and staying aligned with your core truth, might trigger your loved ones or it may inspire them. Sometimes both. So perhaps it's time to be the change you want to see in your relationships. As you live a life that's aligned, others will naturally respond to your resonance.

The things you once thought were a problem are no longer a problem

As we evolve, so do our ideas. So perhaps we were fixated on what felt like a problem. But by doing the work, that fixation becomes acceptance. We realise we've got our needs covered and we're filling our own cup.

We no longer take people's actions so personally

We start to recognise that the way people behave is a reflection of what's happening for them on the inside, rather than of what's happening with us. That doesn't make bad behaviour okay, but it certainly takes out the sting and gives us perspective. When we don't take it personally, we're less likely to be pulled into drama. We stay aligned in our truth and centred in our lane.

We realise it's not our business to ask them to change

Just because we want someone to change doesn't mean they have to. By accepting them for who they are and the choices they make, we are more likely to connect authentically. Ultimately, embracing a commitment to inner growth means embracing the isness of what life presents to us. This might mean riding the waves that will inevitably come when our loved ones don't fit the ideal of who and what we want. This involves learning when it's our place to accept a loved one's life choices.

We recognise what we can't accept

The more we get to know ourselves, the more we get to love ourselves. As we grow in self-love, we become increasingly aware of the impact our relationships have on us. We start to draw stronger boundaries around toxic and negative relationships. While I mentioned above that we need to accept our loved ones, this comes with a caveat: we also learn to recognise what we can't accept. These are our personal deal breakers and non-negotiables.

Toxicity can show up in relationships in myriad ways. Sometimes the signs are more obvious – physical abuse, emotional abuse, betrayal, dishonesty or disregard – but sometimes they are harder to identify, showing up as a very subtle feeling you have in someone's company. Toxicity isn't always about what it looks like, but often what it feels like, deep down. Gut feelings are our guardian angels.

Sometimes a relationship is unhealthy because of a person's behaviour, and sometimes it's no-one's fault. It's simply that you've changed, or they've changed. When we grow, we may grow out of certain dynamics that are no longer a match.

Some of our relationships may need to end, take space, or change. Sometimes conflict isn't an opportunity, it's downright damaging. Sometimes the most harmonious move is to let the relationship die in its current form.

This may look like a drastic change or shake-up – perhaps you move out of the house you share, or create strong boundaries around the way you interact. Or maybe it's time to end the relationship, either for a time or forever.

We often know deep down if this needs to be – usually before we're ready to openly acknowledge it. Learning to listen to our intuition and acting from our inner truth requires us to trust ourselves.

NOTE: This can be especially challenging if the person you no longer feel aligned with is a family member. Please be sure to remind yourself that just because someone is family doesn't give them the right to treat you as less than what you deserve.

NOTE: It can also be especially challenging if you dearly love the person you need space from or are moving on from. You can love someone and still have to let them go. You can understand the reasons behind someone's toxic behaviour and still choose to not accept it.

8: MAKING CHANGE

'Maintaining your energy is more important than fighting to be understood by people who aren't interested in understanding you.'

The right people for you show up

On the flip side, as you become more aligned with your true self, you will start to attract people and circumstances that support your wellbeing. As you change, so does your resonance, which then sends invisible but very real messages to the people and the world around you. Messages like, 'I'm someone who knows my worth. I'm someone who is living my best life. I'm someone who deserves to be prioritised.' The universe is listening.

Selecting your inner circle

The people you surround yourself with create the shape of your life. One of the greatest acts of empowerment is to have standards about who you hold close, and to steer clear of toxic communication, unhealthy connections or endless cycles of conflict that do more damage.

Many of us have never considered that it's okay – in fact, it's important – to be selective about who gets our time and energy. But life is too precious to settle for feeling unsettled in our relationships. So whether your circle is small or wide, be sure the people in your life genuinely know, honour and love the true you.

Practice

Next time you catch up with friends or family, consider these questions:

- How do you feel in their company? Do you feel filled up when you walk away? Or drained? Have they given you a boost of love and confidence? Or brought you down?
- How do you act in their company? Do you hold back your opinions, feel overly conscious about what you say, worry about what they'll think, or bend over backwards to please and impress?
- What's the ratio between positive versus negative interactions? If you find that more often than not you don't feel great, it's time to seriously review if this connection is for you.

<u>Practice</u>

Write out the top ten core values of what you seek in your relationships. By getting clear about what we want, we know what to look out for – and what to steer clear of.

1. _____

2. _____

3. _____

4. _____

5. _____

6. _____

7. _____

8. _____

9. _____

10. _____

Planting seeds for personal change

You swear you'll never put yourself in that situation again, or maybe you're determined to do it differently the next time around. Yet somehow the dynamic keeps repeating itself – either with the same person, or in the same scenario with a different face. We repeat what we don't repair.

We do the work, ultimately, by becoming self-aware. By witnessing our patterns, our behaviours, beliefs, stories and emotions. By questioning why we do what we do, reflecting on how we feel and being honest about what we're experiencing. From a place of witness can come the impetus to create shifts in the way we do things and make changes. First we observe, then we take action.

OBSERVE

In Chapter 1, we began the process of observing our emotions, beliefs, stories, projections and shadows. We excavated the heck out of our internal landscape, and got to know ourselves in a more authentic way. Now let's take a look at how our external world is shaping and affecting who we are.

'When you're considering someone as a potential partner or even as a potential friend, instead of focusing on whether you like them or not, a more important question to ask yourself is: "Do I like who I am when I'm around this person?"'

Alison Armstrong

Question

Who are the top five people you spend most of your time with?

1 _____	4 _____
2 _____	5 _____
3 _____	

Do the people on your list reflect your core values? Give a tick next to the ones who do, and a cross next to the ones who don't.

What are some of the stories you tell yourself about relationships?

- 'He's polite, so it's boring.'
- 'All the good ones are taken.'
- 'Relationships are hard work.'
- 'I don't want a relationship right now.'

Do your words align with your core values or true relationship desires?

What is your attitude towards other people who appear to have healthy, harmonious connections? Do you bitch about them? Do you resent them? Are you jealous of them? Are you happy for them?

NOTE: Resonance karma is real. By bitching or resenting them for having the thing you seek, you're energetically repelling the very thing you want.

TAKE ACTION

We create change by choosing not to make the same decisions we made the day before. This may feel a bit weird and uncomfortable. If you're making changes, you're doing things differently. So it's likely you'll be stepping out of your comfort zone and into new territory. Just because it feels different, doesn't mean it's wrong. If you're going to make lasting change and you're re-wiring new habits, then this squeeze shows growth in a new area. Like anything, it will become easier with practise.

Tip

Don't wait to find your new partner or crew. Create space to allow them in. This may feel lonely for a time – you might not date or socialise as much. But when you create the space, you rewrite your resonance and become available for the right people to show up.

Create boundaries around your time and
energy for people who you genuinely can't remove
from your life. This may be your partner's family,
or a colleague in your workplace.

'If you're looking for
meaningful, harmonious,
intimate and conscious
relationships, stop seeing
people who aren't
reflecting that
for you.'

BECOME SELECTIVE ABOUT WHAT YOU FEED YOUR BRAIN

We are deeply affected by external stimuli. It creates our filter of the world. The current world around us is designed to make us feel discontent. So if we aren't conscious and specific about what goes in, it will be chosen for us, likely taking us on a wild ride of insecurity and emptiness.

Question

Which content do you consume the most? Is it podcasts, books, newspapers, reality TV, social media? Write them down. Do these reflect your core values? Give a tick next to the ones that do, and a cross next to the ones that don't.

1 _____

2 _____

3 _____

4 _____

5 _____

OBSERVE YOUR PATTERNS, UNDERSTAND YOUR TRAUMA

Are you attracting the same type of person? Are you experiencing the same types of conflicts? It may be time to do some digging. Looking at your history, past choices, upbringing and life experiences can help to put the puzzle pieces together, helping you understand why you do what you do. For example, I had a friend who desperately wanted to be in a relationship. He had been single for seven years. After going to therapy, he recognised that although he wanted love, due to stories borne from his upbringing, he was actually terrified of love. By doing the work he was able to address trauma he had experienced in childhood and issues he had with his mother. Not long afterwards he met his now-partner.

Tip

In this book we've focused on tools you can use for connecting with others, but it's important to recognise that unresolved trauma dictates much of how we relate, and will have us repeating patterns until we address it. Understanding how your past is informing your present is more important than any connection tool I can give you. If we don't get to the source, then all we're doing is slapping bandaids over deep wounds.

I highly recommend working with therapists that practice trauma-informed therapy, even if you don't consider yourself to have obvious 'trauma'. Both personal therapists and marriage therapists can offer game-changing guidance in navigating our experience of both past and current relationships.

SPEND TIME WITH PEOPLE WHO ARE SUCCESSFUL IN THE AREA THAT YOU DESIRE

Approach learning new ways of relating in the same way you would learn a new skill. Start with research. If you want to call in a harmonious partnership, for example, spend time with couples who you know are experiencing – and consciously working at – these relationships. Observe how they interact, and ask them questions about how they relate, how they manage conflict and what they equate their success to. Remember, we're not taught relationship skills, but they are skills we can learn.

Practice

Let's ask and answer some honest questions.
Find yourself a quiet space and a comfortable
place to sit. Before you begin, close your eyes
and take three deep breaths (like the practice
on page 157). This will help centre your body
and focus your mind. Then open your eyes
and read the first question. Before answering
it, pause. Close your eyes again, and let the
answer come to you. Don't try to 'think' up
the answer; let it reveal itself. Then write it
down and move to the next question.

- What experiences do I want to stay away
  from, in order to create change?
- Which of my behaviours do I want to change?
- What emotions/stories do I want to re-write?
- What is the new story?
- What/who do I need to let go of in my life?
- What new choices will I make/not make from
  this point onwards?

Start small or go hard. You'll know what's
right for you.

Now, just for fun, pop back to the list of core
values you wrote out. Read through this list
again: does it remind you of someone?

Yep, you're right: it's you. Most likely, you've listed who you are or who you're growing into – which tells me you think you're a pretty awesome human. I agree!

NOTE: Make this list your personal focus. When you amplify these traits within yourself, you grow your resonance in this area. So if, on your list, you're looking for relationships that are adventurous, off you go! Climb a mountain. You're more likely to meet your bestie at the top rather than in a busy city bar.

Doing the work welcomes a wave of emotions. It can be lonely when you lose connections along the way, and sometimes frustrating in those times where you can't share your breakthroughs with your loved ones. Because while you're levelling up to help level up your relationships, you can't assume others will automatically walk the long roads with you.

But that's okay. Ultimately, you're working on you, for you. Your focus – and your job – is on evolving. On going within and shaking up things that no longer serve you. Keep questioning, expanding and shedding the old ways. Your energy introduces you before words do, and as you live from your true self, you create space for others around you to do the same.

8: MAKING CHANGE

Conclusion

Our hearts hum when our relationships are in harmony. As we reach the end of our road together, my hope is that you won't stop singing during the tough times.

By staying conscious during conflict, we allow our relationships to expose our core and reveal our tremendous capacity for love. We create a safe space to be challenged and to challenge our loved ones. We bravely move beyond our conditioning and into a new realm of self-awareness because we know we've got each other's back. Disagreements are no longer disasters. They're opportunities to transform and move forward.

Close your eyes, take a deep breath in, then out. This simple act of stopping, slowing and becoming aware instantly creates space. Can you feel it? This, dear reader, is consciousness. I trust our time together has invited space in. You can access this space by pausing during arguments, acts of ego and negative thoughts. Bad days and difficult phases will still exist, but now you'll be able to apply your tools and move forward. These glimmers make way for relational gold.

We've covered a lot of ground and it will take a lot of practise – and, yes, some mistakes – to integrate these concepts. Be compassionate with yourself. It takes time to settle into a new way of being, and to elevate to a new human being.

Remember that growth doesn't only happen when you close your eyes to meditate or unroll your yoga mat. There's an invitation in the everyday moments. It's here, it's now. Find opportunities to bloom in simple exchanges. Perhaps you start a difficult conversation gently or, mid-disagreement, you step in and self-regulate. Maybe you hold off on making a nasty comment that will hit your partner where it hurts. Or you celebrate a small win after an uncomfortable interaction – even if it doesn't go perfectly.

You have set out on your path of self-discovery. This is a great place for us to end our journey, because the greatest step you can take towards finding harmony in your relationships is to make peace within yourself. As we get to know ourselves, we get to know our loved ones on a deeper level. By walking a more intimate path together, we're more connected and less conflicted. And that's something to sing about.

Go well, soul seeker.

Thank yous and Acknowledgements

I would like to acknowledge the Traditional Custodians of the land on which I wrote these words, the Gunditjmara people of the Gadubanud lands. I pay my respects to ancestors and Elders, past and present.

To Alice and the Hardie Grant team. Thank you for trusting me, once again, with my vision for this book. It's been a dream to work with a team that is committed to creating change and positively impacting lives.

Thank you to Libby Turner, for taking this work when it was a jumble of pieces and helping me shape and develop it. You brought fresh ideas, teased out the goodness and offered wisdom and perspective.

To my writing coach Jenna Meade. For lighting up my words and helping me refine these pages. Your edits, notes and additions have been priceless to this final version. I can't imagine doing this without you.

To the huge community of workshop participants and clients that I've worked with over the past decade. Thank you for trusting me with the challenges you've faced in your connections. Nothing has been more rewarding than to witness marriages bounce back from the brink of divorce, individuals heal long-term resentments, families reconcile, and people walk away from toxic relationships not aligned with their deepest truth. Thank you for digging deep, and finding gold. It takes true bravery to show up like that.

Thank you to my parents and Clare, for being by my side while I wrote these words, helping me chase a three year old, nurse a baby and survive on very little sleep. I couldn't have done this without you and coffee.

Finally, to my husband, Nootsie. To the moments when our love has gone south. Thank you for working with me to transmute our breakdowns into breakthroughs. I'm grateful for the way our hard times have grown us. Thank you for reading every word of this book and putting the tools to the test.

FURTHER READING

You'll find articles and recommended reading on my website www.emmapower.com, all designed with you in mind. Be in touch for more information on upcoming courses and offerings.

 @emma_power

Published in 2022 by Hardie Grant Books, an imprint of Hardie Grant Publishing

Hardie Grant Books (Melbourne)
Wurundjeri Country
Building 1, 658 Church Street
Richmond, Victoria 3121

Hardie Grant Books (London)
5th & 6th Floors
52–54 Southwark Street
London SE1 1UN
hardiegrantbooks.com

A catalogue record for this book is available from the National Library of Australia

When Love Goes South
ISBN 9781743797631
10 9 8 7 6 5 4 3 2 1

Commissioning Editor: Alice Hardie-Grant
Editor: Vanessa Lanaway
Design Manager: Kristin Thomas
Designer: Studio Polka
Production Manager: Todd Rechner

Colour reproduction by Splitting Image Colour Studio
Printed in China by Leo Paper Products LTD.

MIX
Paper from responsible sources
FSC® C020056

Hardie Grant acknowledges the Traditional Owners of the country on which we work, the Wurundjeri people of the Kulin nation and the Gadigal people of the Eora nation, and recognises their continuing connection to the land, waters and culture. We pay our respects to their Elders past, present and emerging.